Frustration

Mary Jaye Moore

"All art is pain suffered and outlived" - Robert Hayden

"Pain breeds art. Its inevitability gives art its eternity." - Mary Jaye Moore

Take a look inside this frustrated mind. See the frustrations of life wreak havoc in real time. This book contains poems about depression, suicidal ideation, hope, sadness, loss of faith, and much more. At first glance, this book may look like wreckage. Similar to how I feel, it may look like everything is falling apart. But I believe it is falling into place. I believe my past, my old emotions, and my old self are falling away to create something new and beautiful. But before beauty can form, the falling must take place. And that's what this is, part of the falling, part of the breaking, part of the process before the rebuilding. I tried to have the fake smiles and the false hope to get me by but I noticed there was no growth. I noticed, I didn't experience growth in the pretending but in the lamenting. I saw it in the crying, I saw it in the times I allowed myself to be sad. I saw it when I acknowledged my emotions and admitted I was angry and frustrated. The real work could begin after that. Daily, I feel like I could die in this process, but I renew my mind and patiently wait for some resolve. I patiently wait for the pressure to be lifted. As I wait, my mind and body seem to be under arrest, but my pen remains free. It has allowed me to write about these emotions, and the farewells to my past self. I hope every reader enjoys these pieces about this piece of my life.

-   MJM

For the people who think their stories have ended because their current chapter isn't pretty. There's always more.

I resented my elders for not teaching me the ways of the fickle thing we call life. I realized, even they couldn't have prepared me for this.

-   surviving

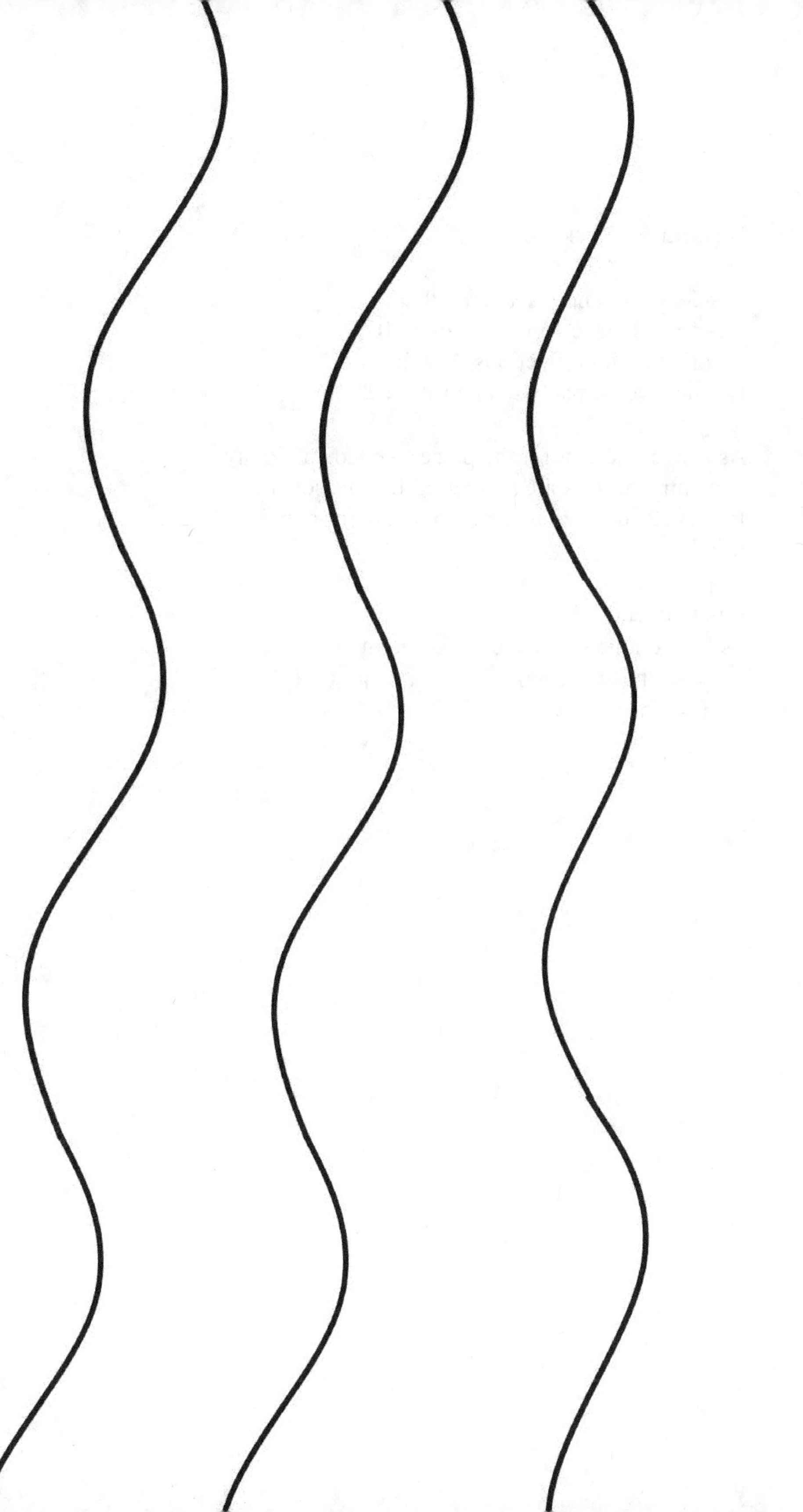

Welcome to Rock Bottom

I broke down and discovered there
was a place beneath rock bottom. It
was filled with reflections. My flaws
laid uncovered ready to be dissected.

As my resentment for the place swelled so did my
contentment. Despite my hatred for this sorrow-
filled palace, I saw generational burdens being
lifted.

I met my darkness.
Its hold on me was vicious. At first it was a
nuisance but the deeper I got the more I felt its
chains loosen.

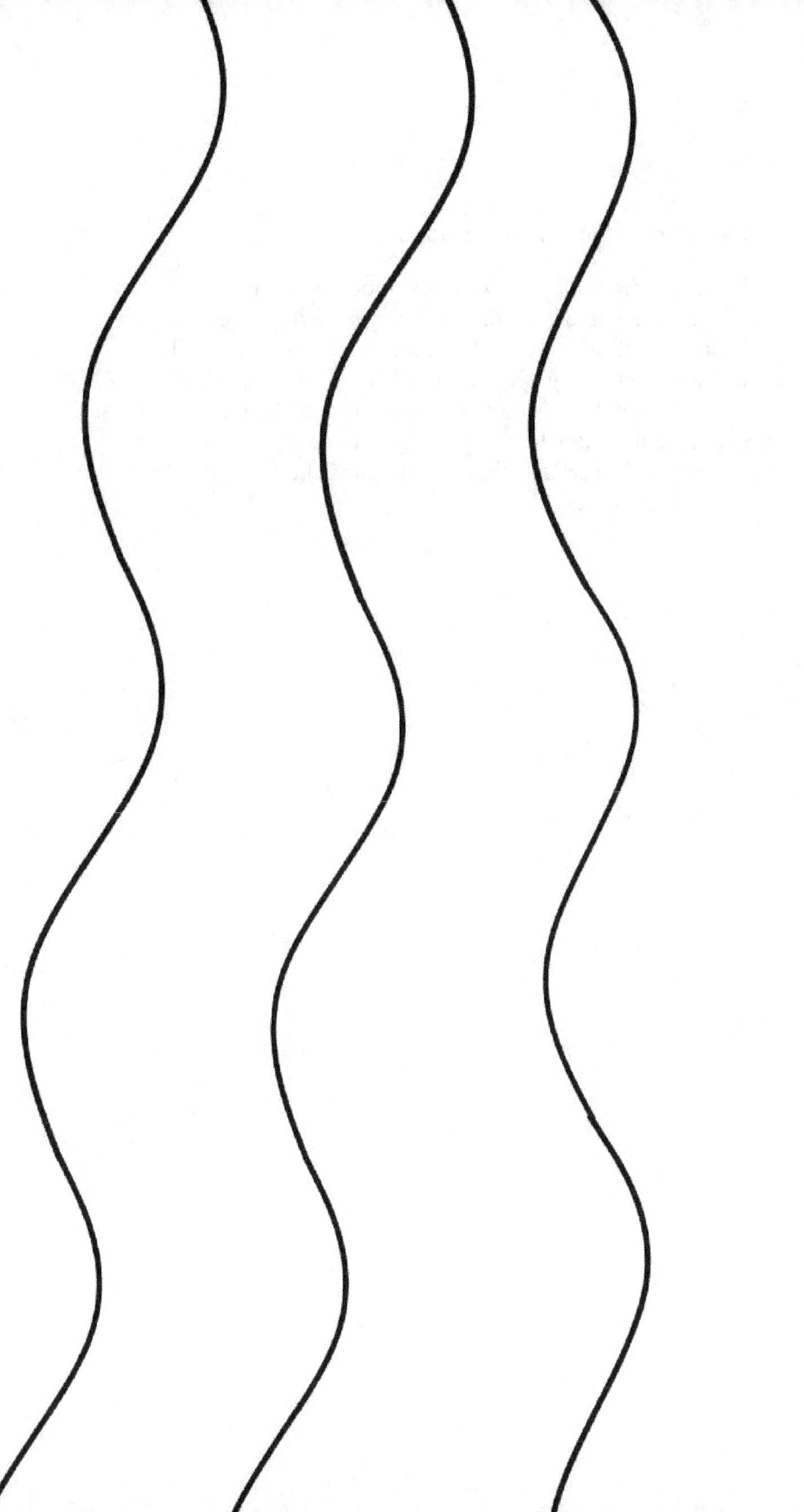

I wish I could mourn in the morning

I wish the tears that fell when the moon and stars were shining, appeared after the sun had finished rising. I wish my depression didn't cower. I wish it had the courage to show its face when all eyes were on me. Instead, it waits until the only thing looking is darkness. It waits until help is far gone and no matter how loud my wails are, they will be left unanswered. It waits until the only thing there to catch my tears are pillows.

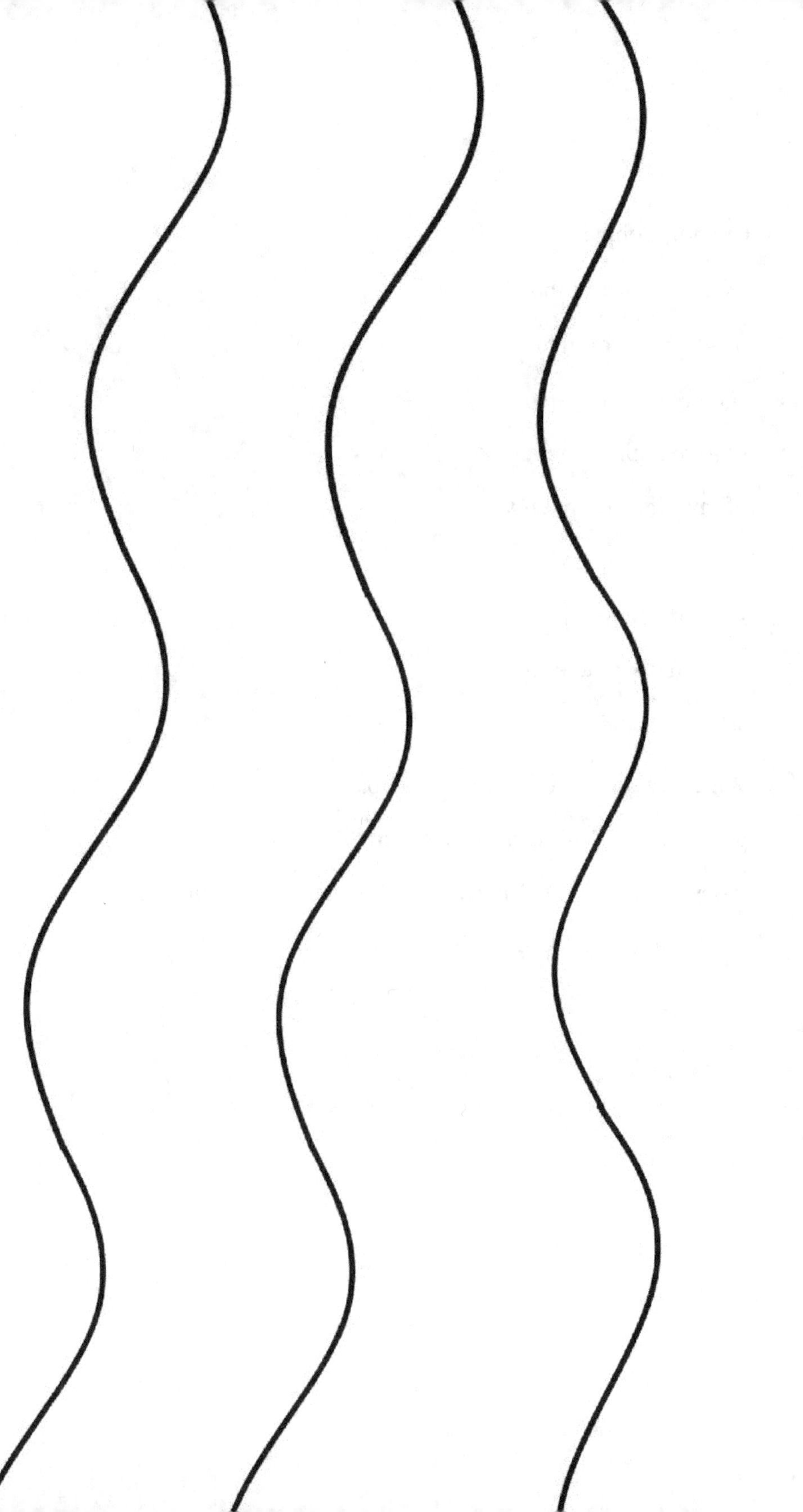

Craving Company

I see company as this

bright beam of light

and being alone dims it.

I thrive in the dimming

of myself, and I put my

need for company on a

shelf and I glory in

never needing to even

ask for a hand to help.

But every now and then I hear company's voice in the

distance, and I'm eager to listen, so I pause my

independence. Now I'm ear to wall forming my opinion on

conversations my voice will never get to be in.

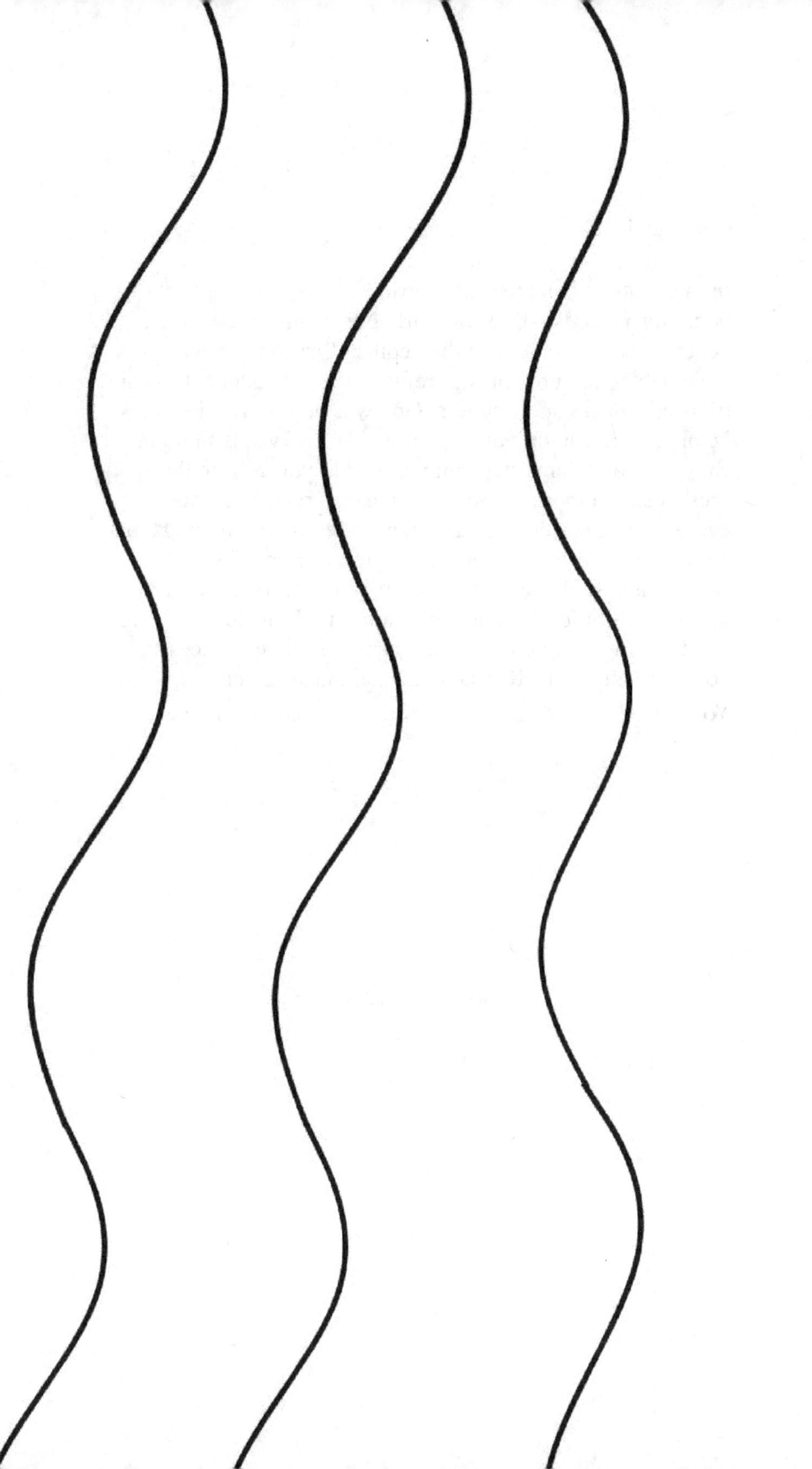

Come undone

In moments of laughter only a grin is present. In the heat of your anger words fail to walk off your tongue but the tears never cease to run. And in the depths of frustration and undeniable pressure you still refuse to come undone. In your trials of sadness and sickness, God was your only witness. A helping hand couldn't attest, because in every situation you were the good Samaritan coming to help yourself. In the presence of company, you act as the observer. You notice every change of emotion, the fake smiles covering things that are broken and your ear is tuned to the warning signs of commotion. In the face of freedom, you refuse its invitation because inhibition is your habitation. In this analogy you are the dam waiting to burst. In this human life the chances of you allowing yourself to be human are next to none.

You can hear your inner being screaming, come undone!

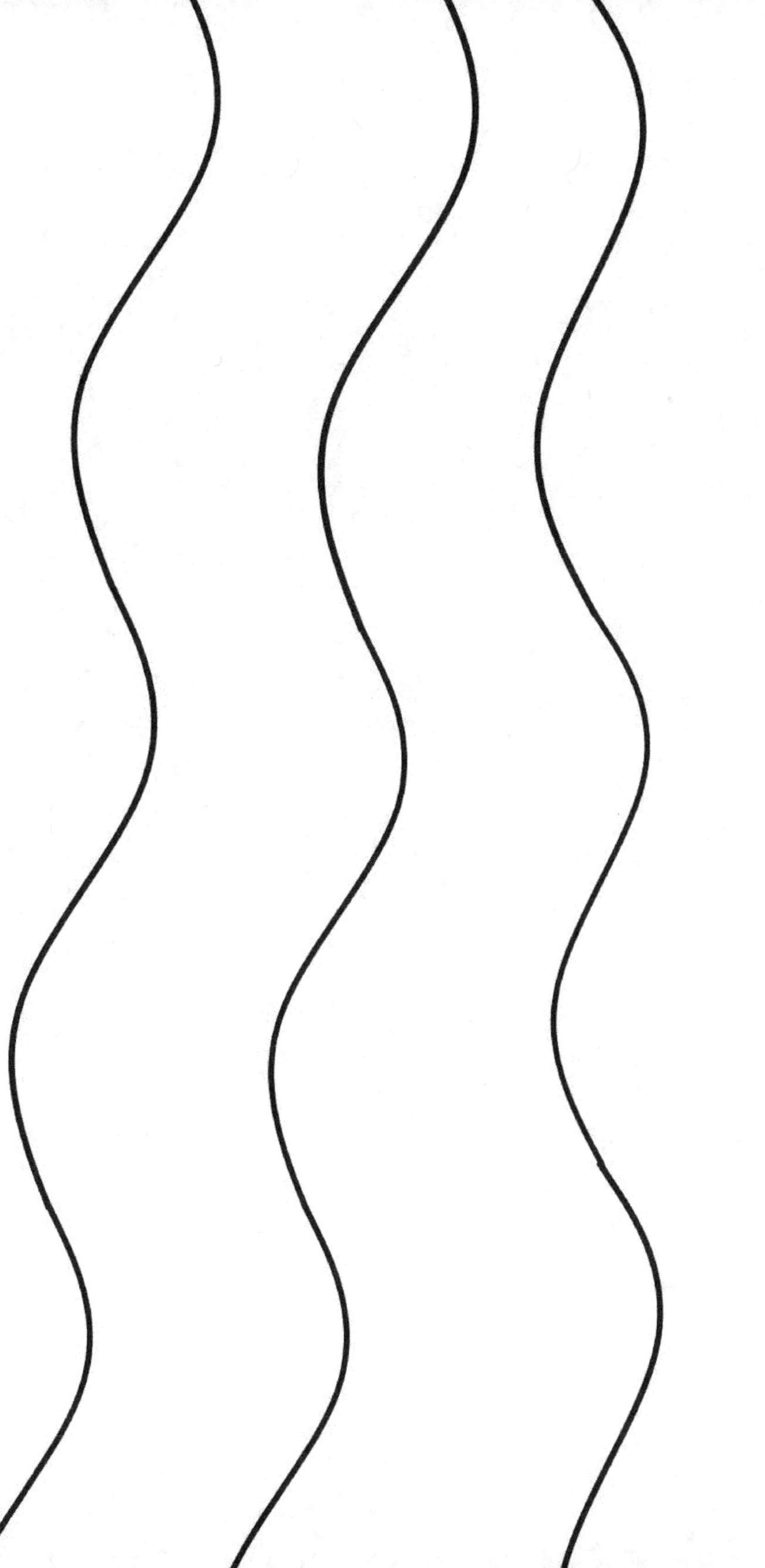

"I'm okay."

- lies I've told

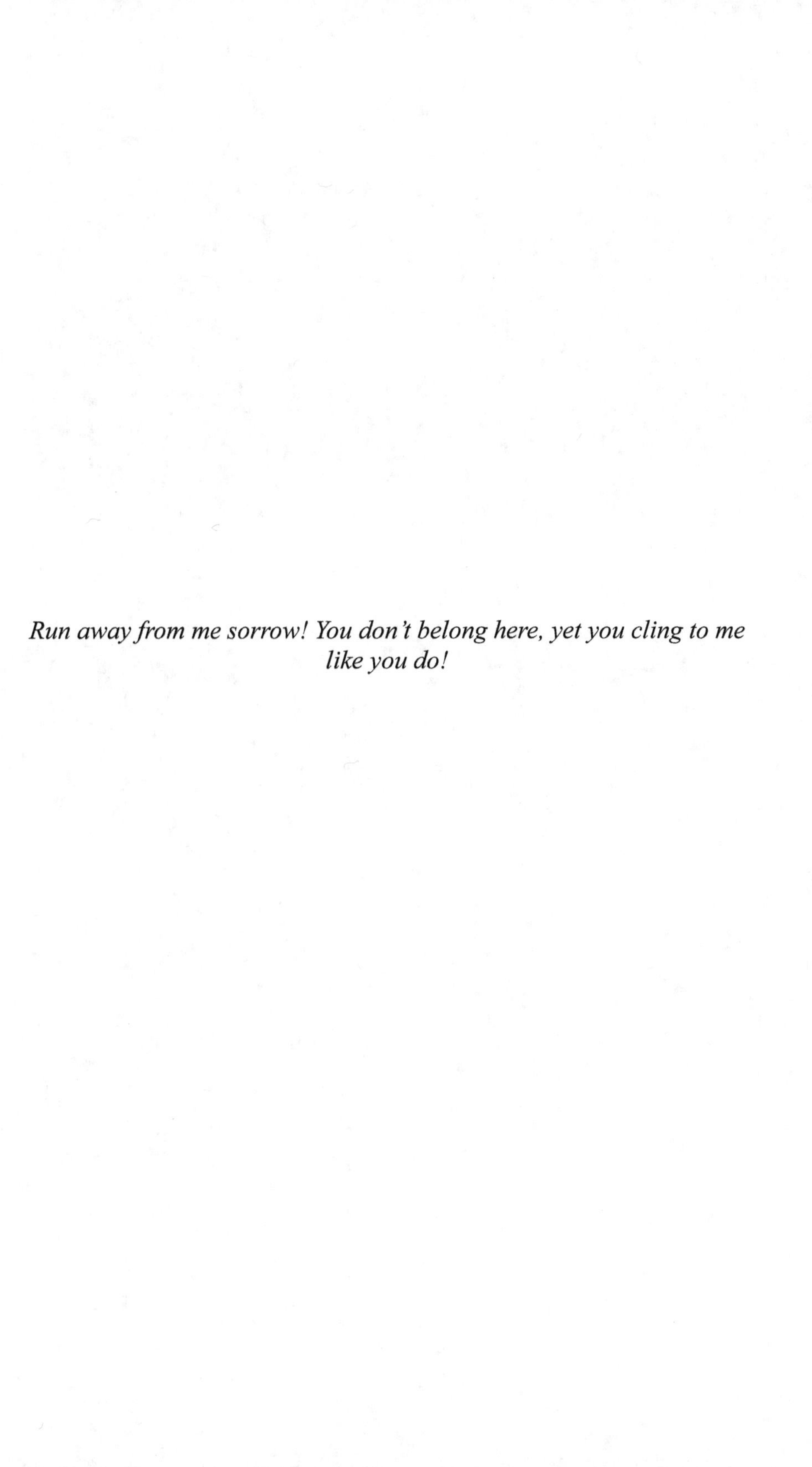

*Run away from me sorrow! You don't belong here, yet you cling to me
like you do!*

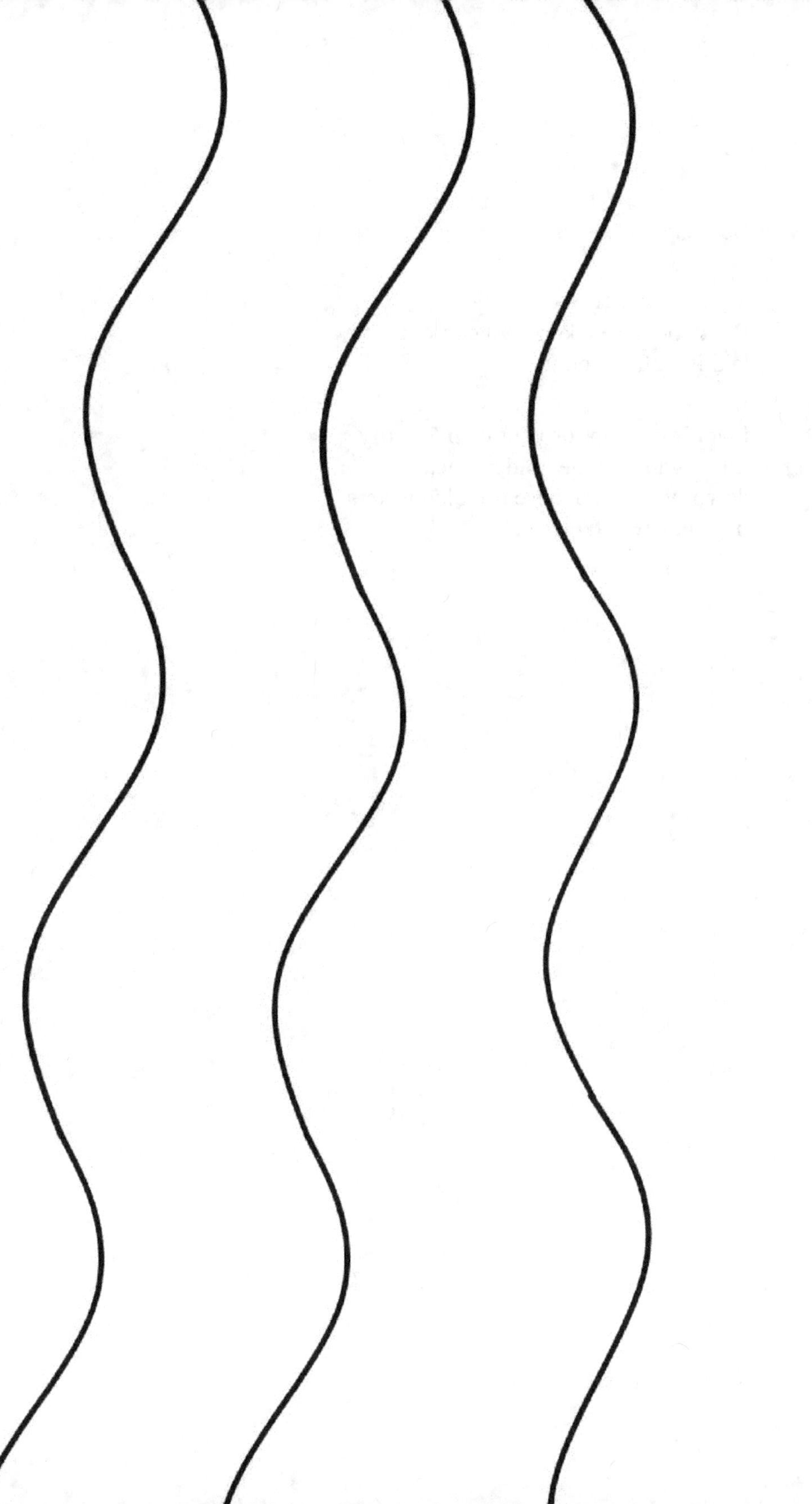

Dear God

My arms are crossed.
I'm done. I've taken my heart out. I've
laid it on the ground.

I won't look up for your help, but my
pride won't let me hold my head
down. Why send these troubled waters
if you knew I'd drown?

Breathe into me

Wake me up!
I lay here lifeless, hoping I could awake and live!
I'm envious of Adam. Breathe into me with the same
devotion you had with him. Become my barterer. Take
these ashes and give me beauty!

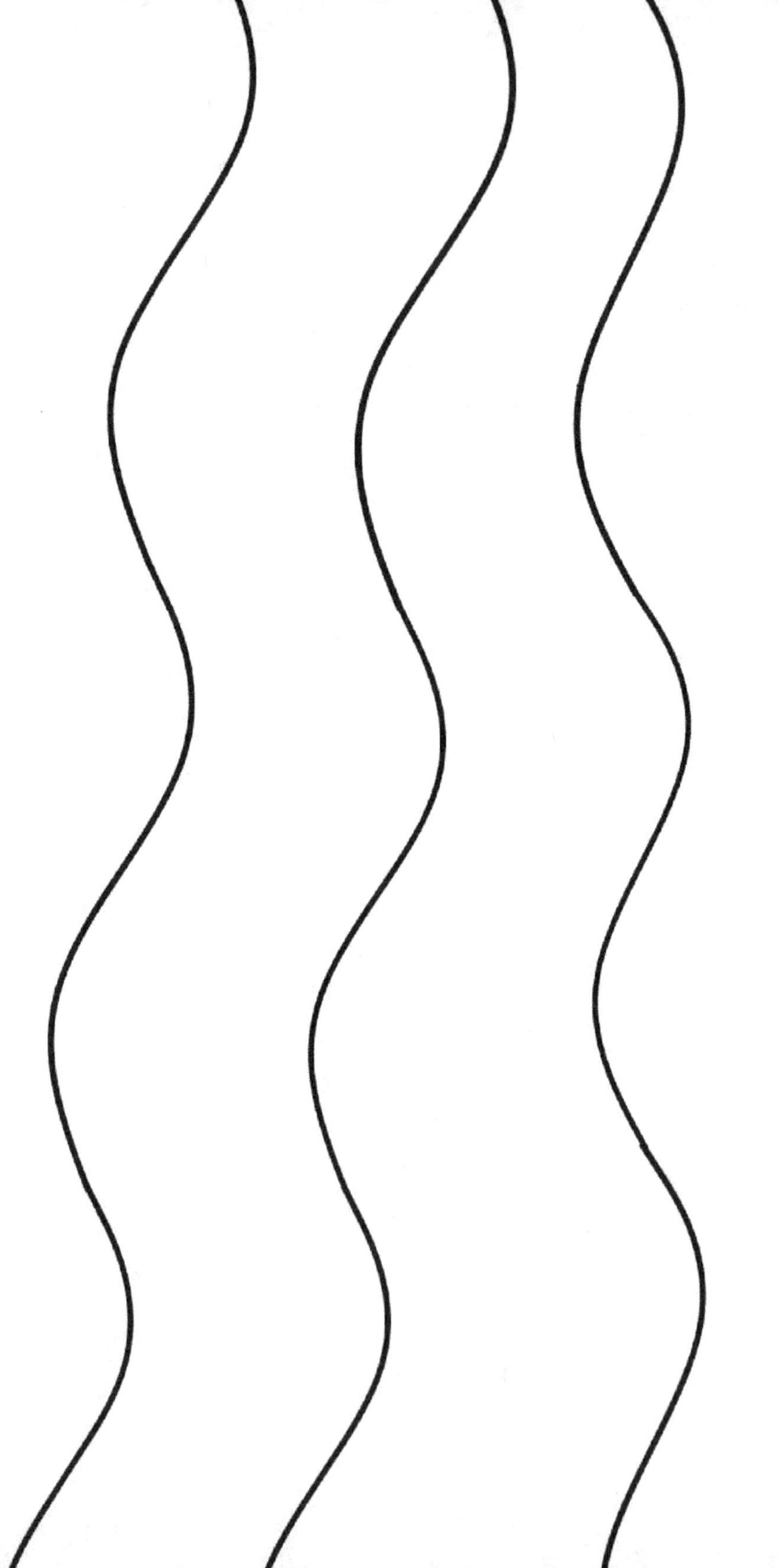

Bitter

This bitterness is my shame!
This anger is the garden that
bloomed from the seeds of pain.
From its harvest, for years
I've abstained, but now I consume its fruits
with no meaning to repent.
My words have become venom and I have no
regards on whom or where I spit!
This rage and I have walked the aisle
and said our vows.
This unholy matrimony was
something I used to resent, but now
it clings to me like our union was
meant to be.

4 Questions

Joy, why do you hate me?
Peace, why do you hide your face from me?
Faith, why do you tease me with your fruits?
Doubt, why am I so drawn to you?

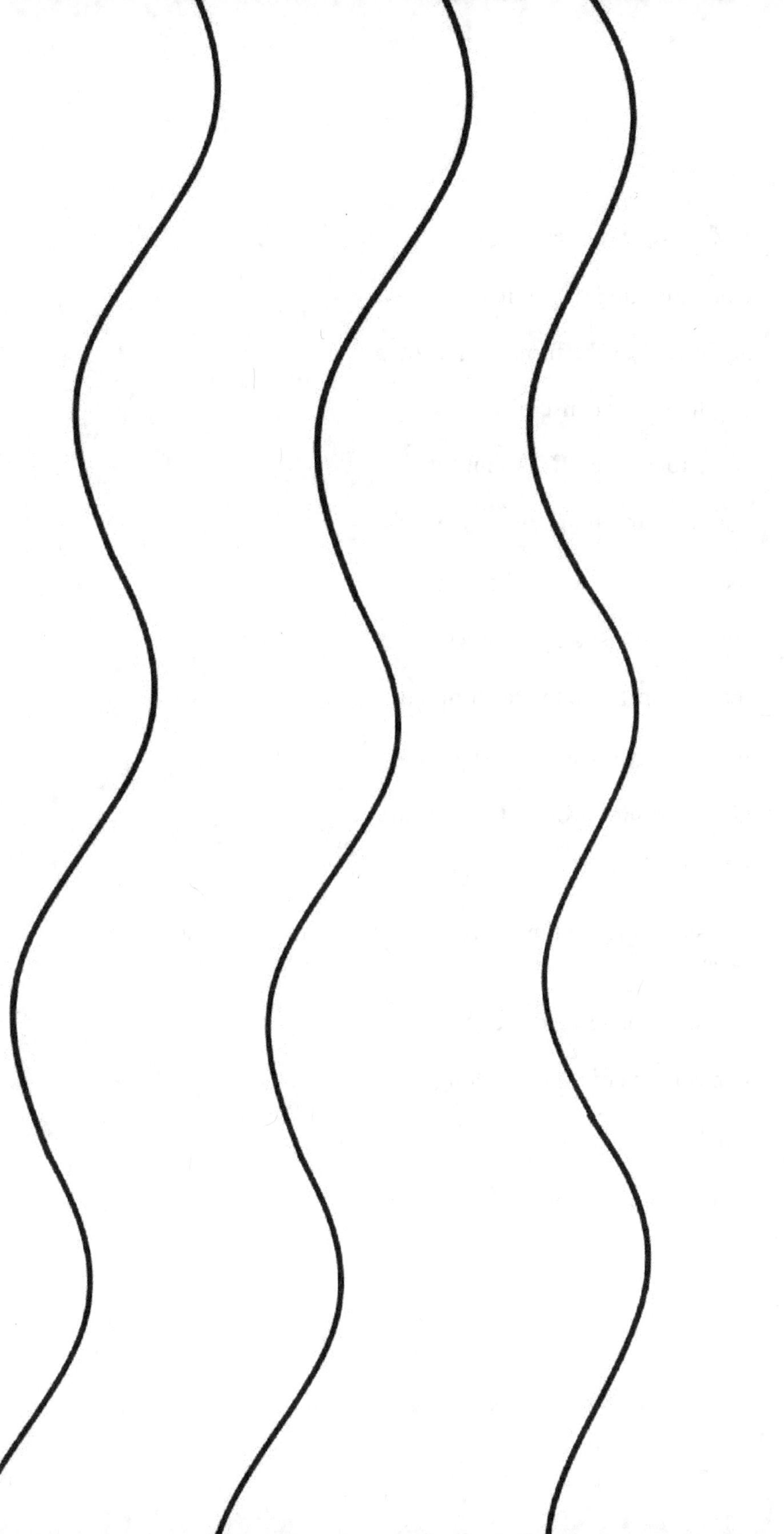

Wide awake (no rest)

Good morning world, it's me

again…. I awake from dreams of

the things my conscious mind

seeks to escape. Eyes shut for

hours but my mind never slowed

its pace. It was awake before the

sun. Anxiety sits on my chest but

that doesn't stop the repetition of

these weary breaths.

Good morning world, it's me again….

I feel like I'm living life on repeat.

I'm surviving off limited rest, constant commotion, and little
peace.

My agitation exceeds beyond my

control. It strikes everything big or

small, young and old.

Good morning world, it's me again…

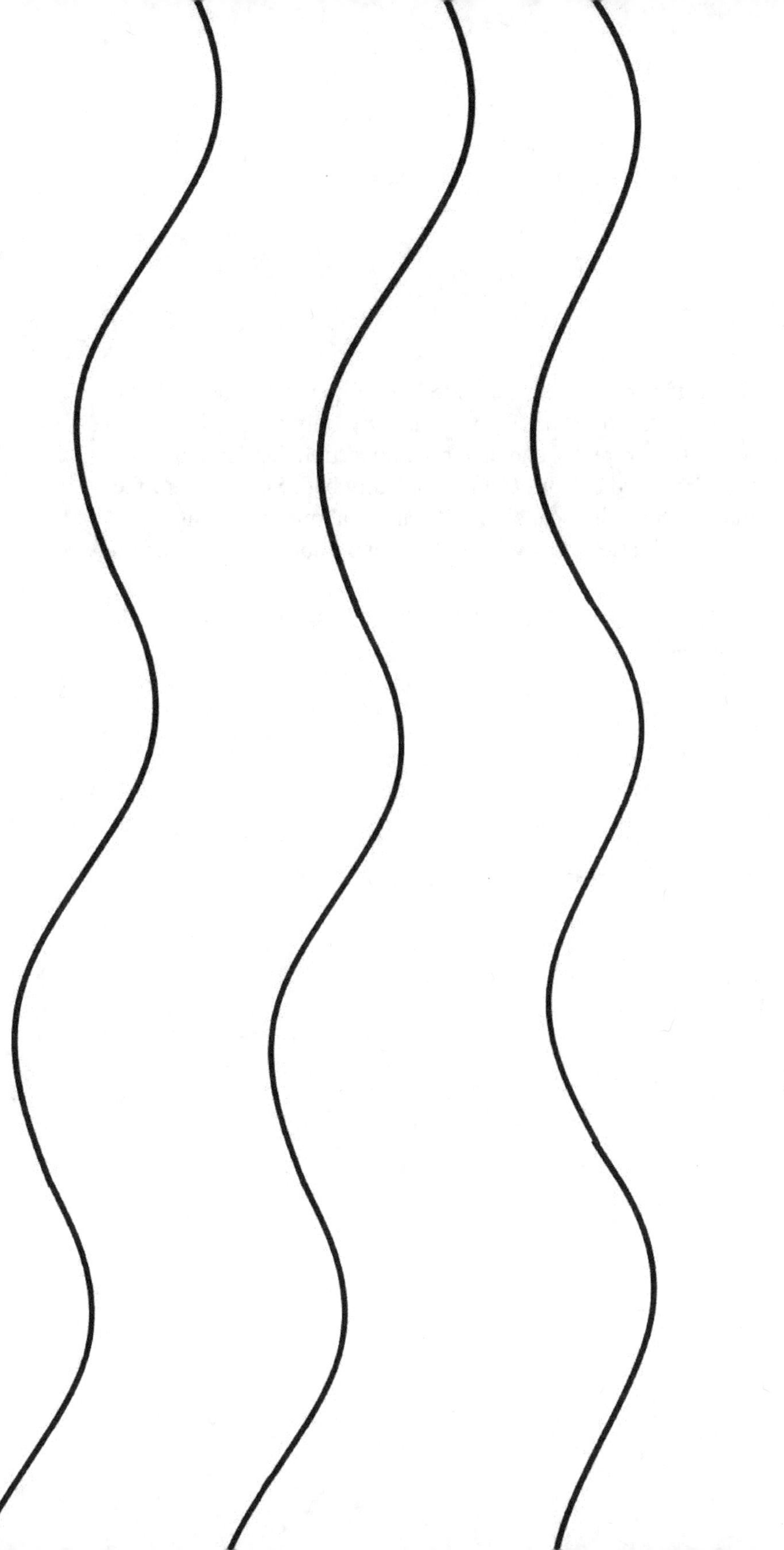

Do you know how hard it is to live a life where you feel like
every decision or move you make will only end up in two
ways, bad or really bad. Then you overthink and discover
there's a third option; Catastrophically bad. Sometimes I feel
like my brain is incapable of thinking about the bright side.
My imagination runs wild as I fantasize about the joys of life.
Then that one small
thought enters and ruins every thought of happiness I could
conjure.

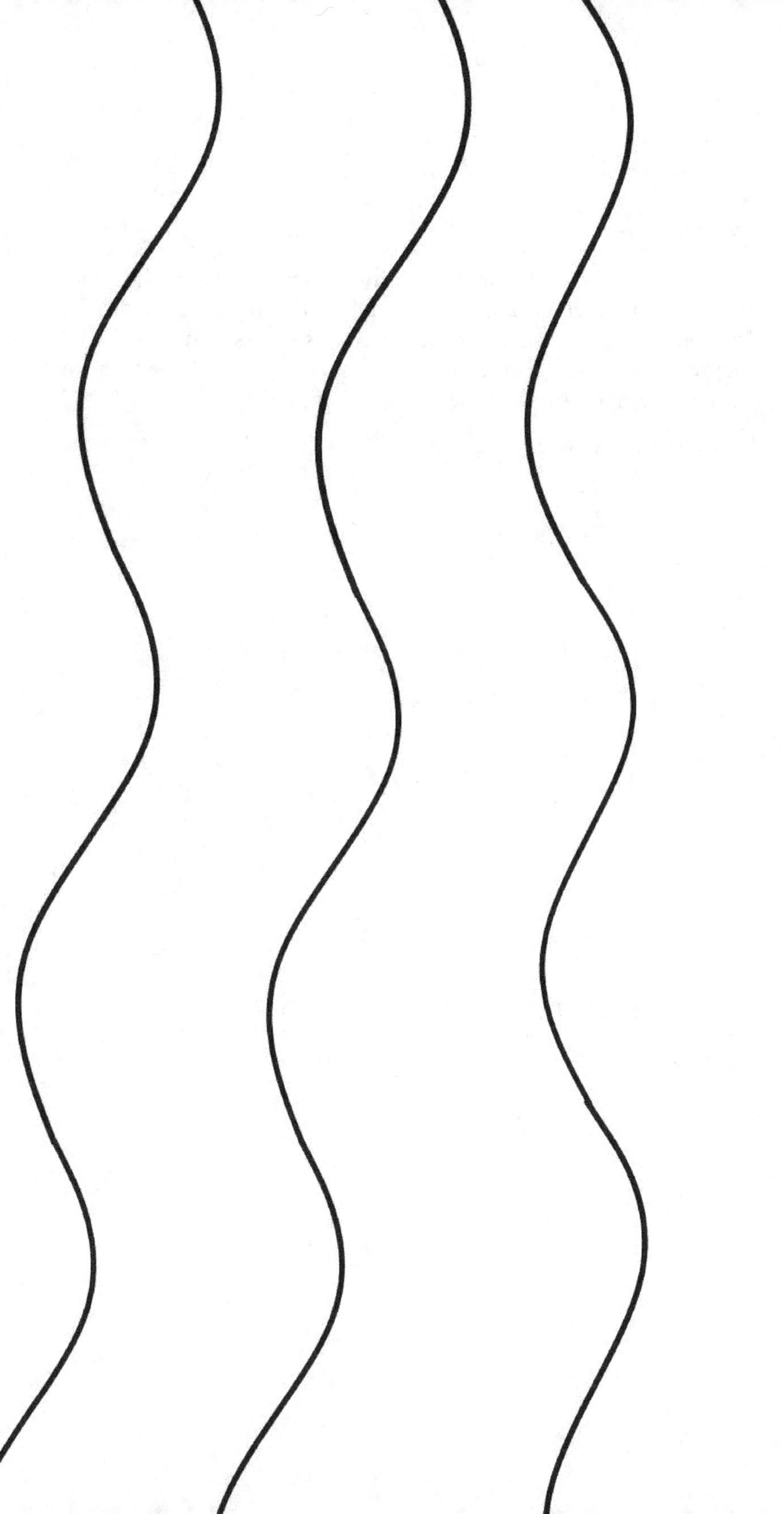

Numb

I'm training myself to not feel. I'd rather become numb than choose to heal. I'd rather experience life with no feelings and disguise it as resiliency. I'd rather not feel because the sadness turns into depression, the anger turns into resentment, and my hope turns into disappointment. And it all leaves me feeling the same.

-      Numb

In this world alone

I screamed it from the mountain top
and got no response.
I left a trail of my tears, yet no one
cared to follow. I retreated, hoping
someone would notice my absence.

Depression played melodies with the
strings of my heart, and I sang its tune
with the power of a full choir, but still,
no one showed up for the show. I feel
as if I am in this world alone and the
only company I keep is sorrow.

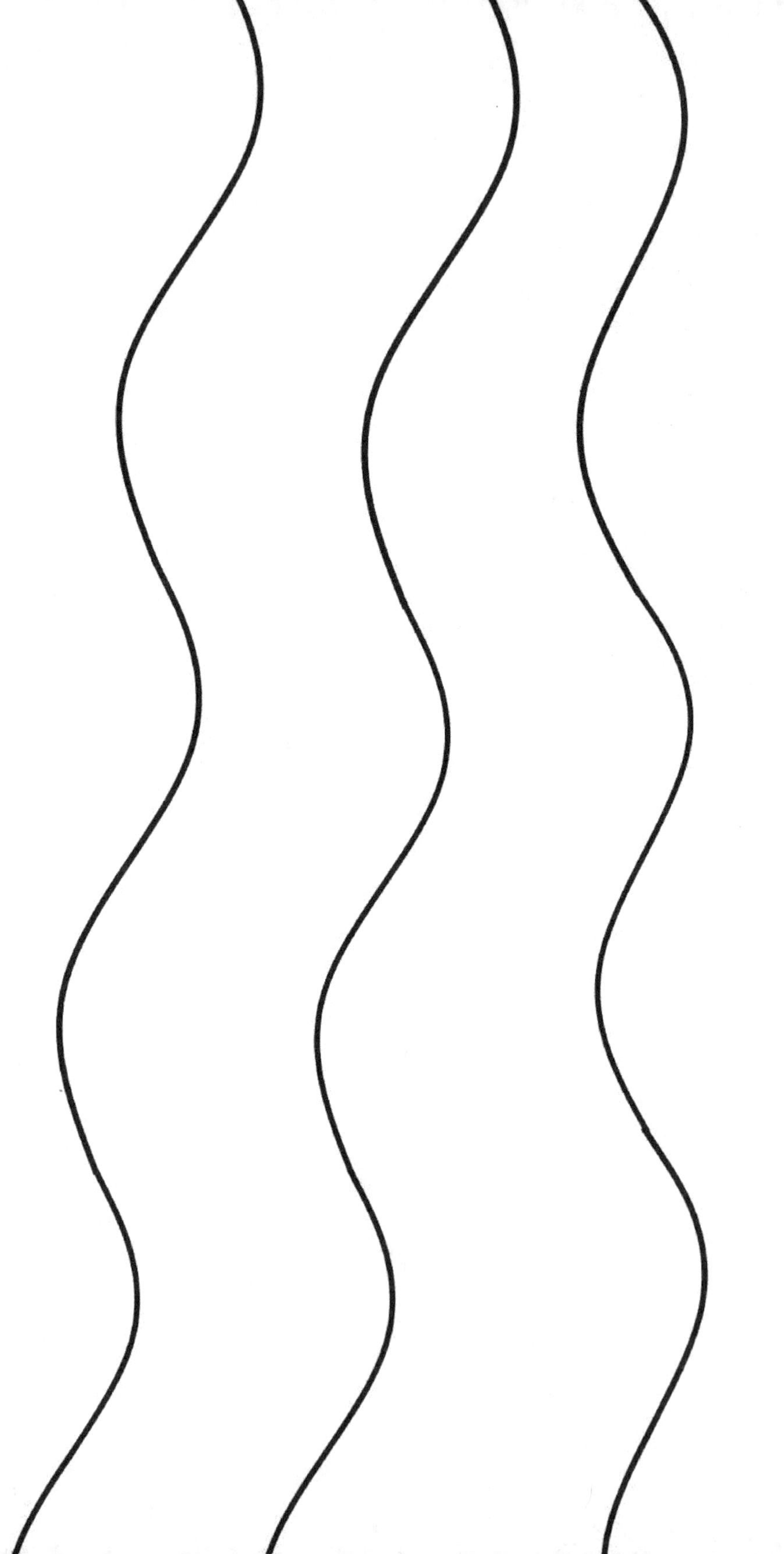

Make me a promise (Make it Matter)

Promise me there is a well!
Promise me it's collecting my tears.
Promise me that there's a harvest!
Promise me my tears are the waters it
needs to bloom. Promise me that soon, I
will eat from its fruits.

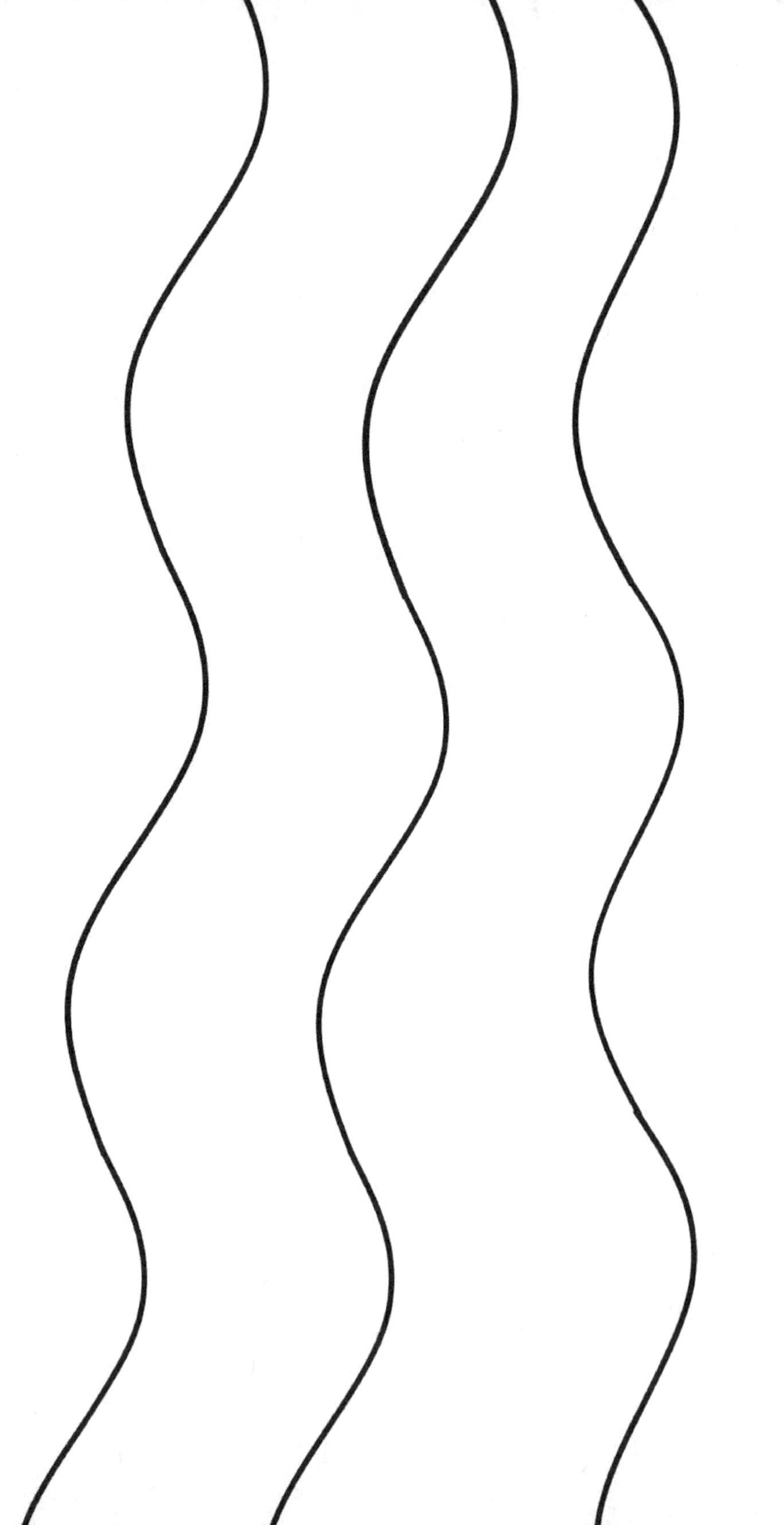

What good is sorry?

Sorry is like stabbing someone in the chest and placing a band aid on it. You don't tend to the wound, and you have no desire to know what comes next.

What good is sorry if you don't change the behavior. Not correcting that behavior is like ripping that band aid off and inserting the knife again. What good is sorry if you just turn around and wound me again? Sorry is the easy way out. Sorry is not enough. Changed behavior is. It's like stitching every inch of the wound together and staying for the healing. Throwing the knife away and anything else that could pierce my heart.

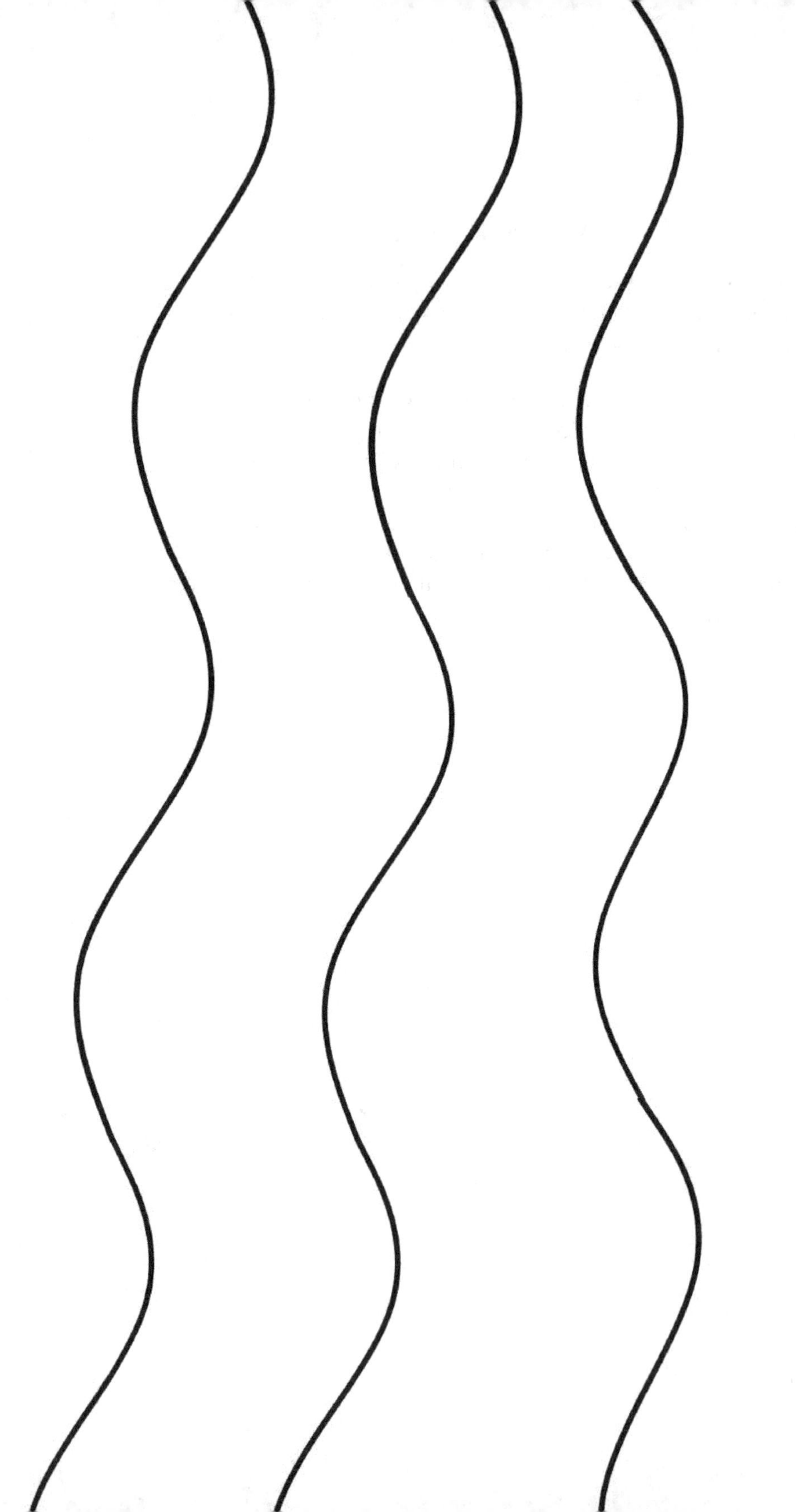

my tears no longer fall at the thought of you.

- that would be my one wish

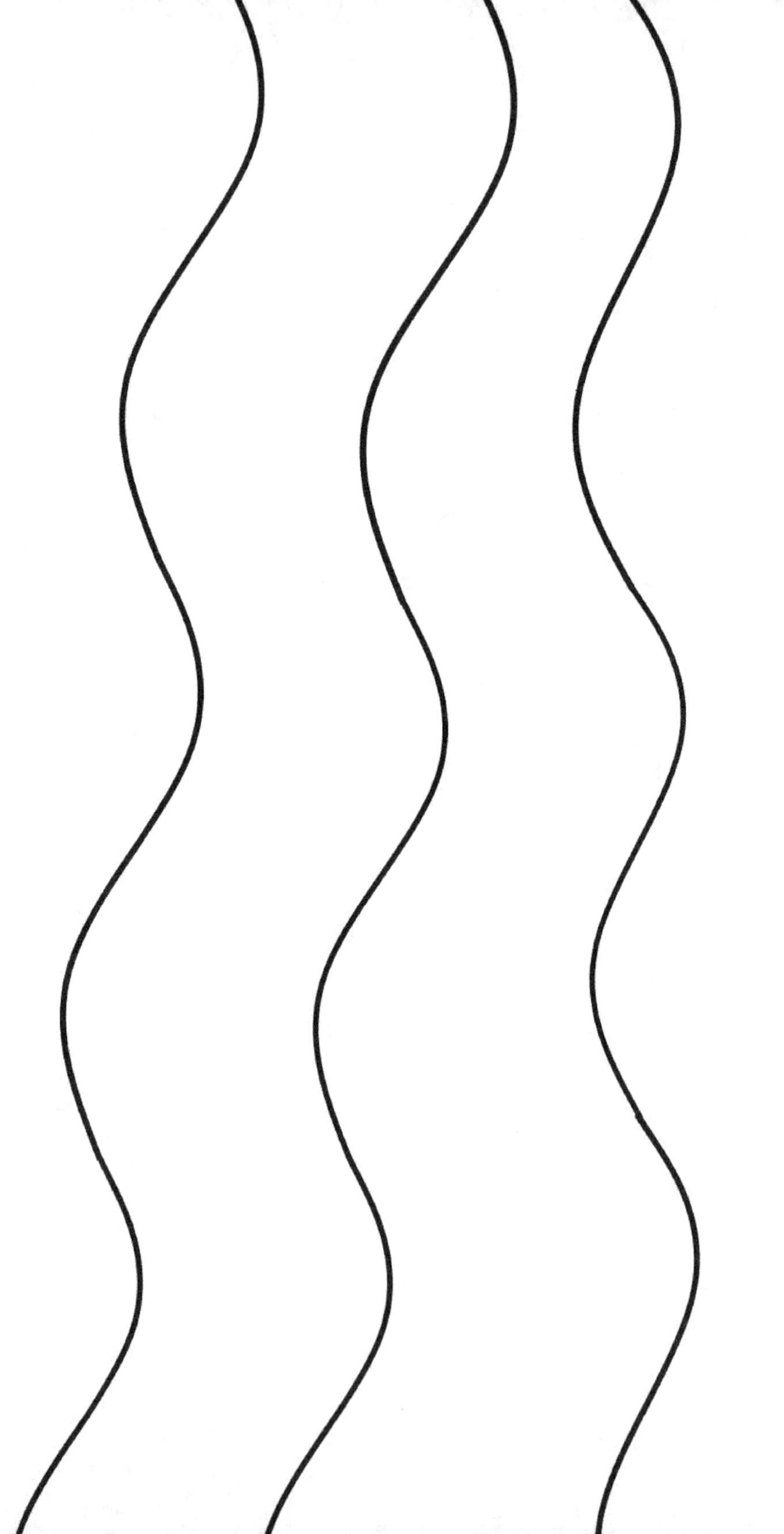

Roaming

Tell me the way home.

I can no longer roam.

My heart is filled with burdens I can no longer hold.

Too heavy to tow on this lonely road.

If only I had someone to help me carry on.

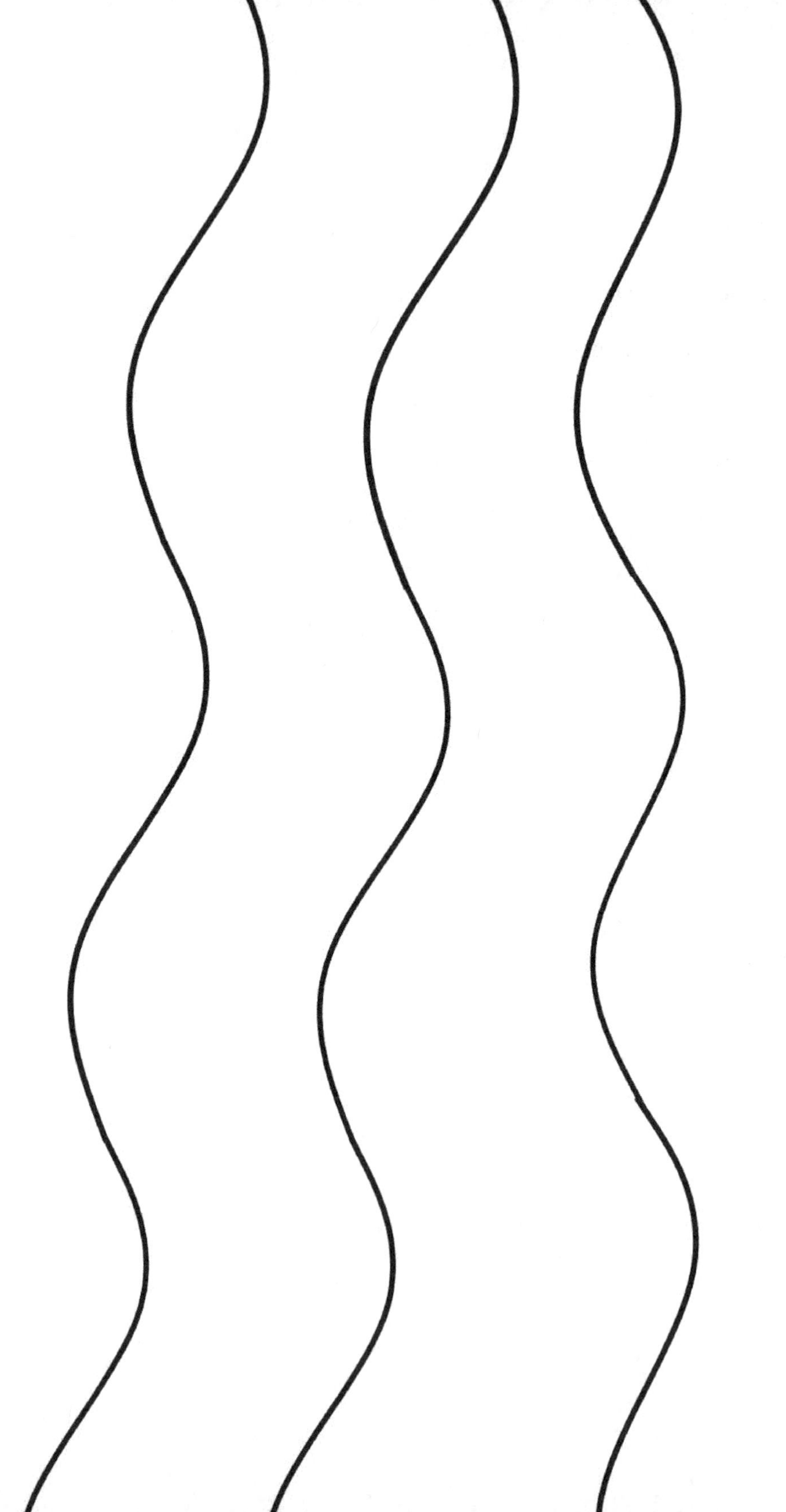

Nightly

I close my eyes but sleep fails to greet me.
Instead, I am met with the night's stillness
provoking my mind to run a race it's prone to lose.
As the echoes of the evening's sighs fill the room,
the memories of the morning's loneliness play on a
loop.

I am able to find peace when I am
reminded that the night's darkness covers
my insecurities, but this silver lining
imposter only leaves me in fear of
morning.

*My ambition and
creativity make promises
but they never keep them.*

\-   *Projects left unfinished;
books left unwritten*

Self-Preservation v. Fear

Self-Preservation and fear are similar beasts but of different natures. Self-Preservation is fervent like a mother's love. It's protection not restriction. Fear is fervent like a storm. It's restriction impersonating protection. Self-Preservation will cause you to run from snakes in the grass. Fear will cause you to run from your destiny.

The poem about the caged bird

She studied each stanza.
Assuming her role as the free bird.
Her inhibition would say otherwise.
Many sang the song of freedom.
She never knew she'd be added to the choir.
Caged bird, caged bird.
She spent her adolescence obsessed with Maya and her words. Didn't yet see them as prophecies.
She didn't know that she would one day find out why the caged bird sings.

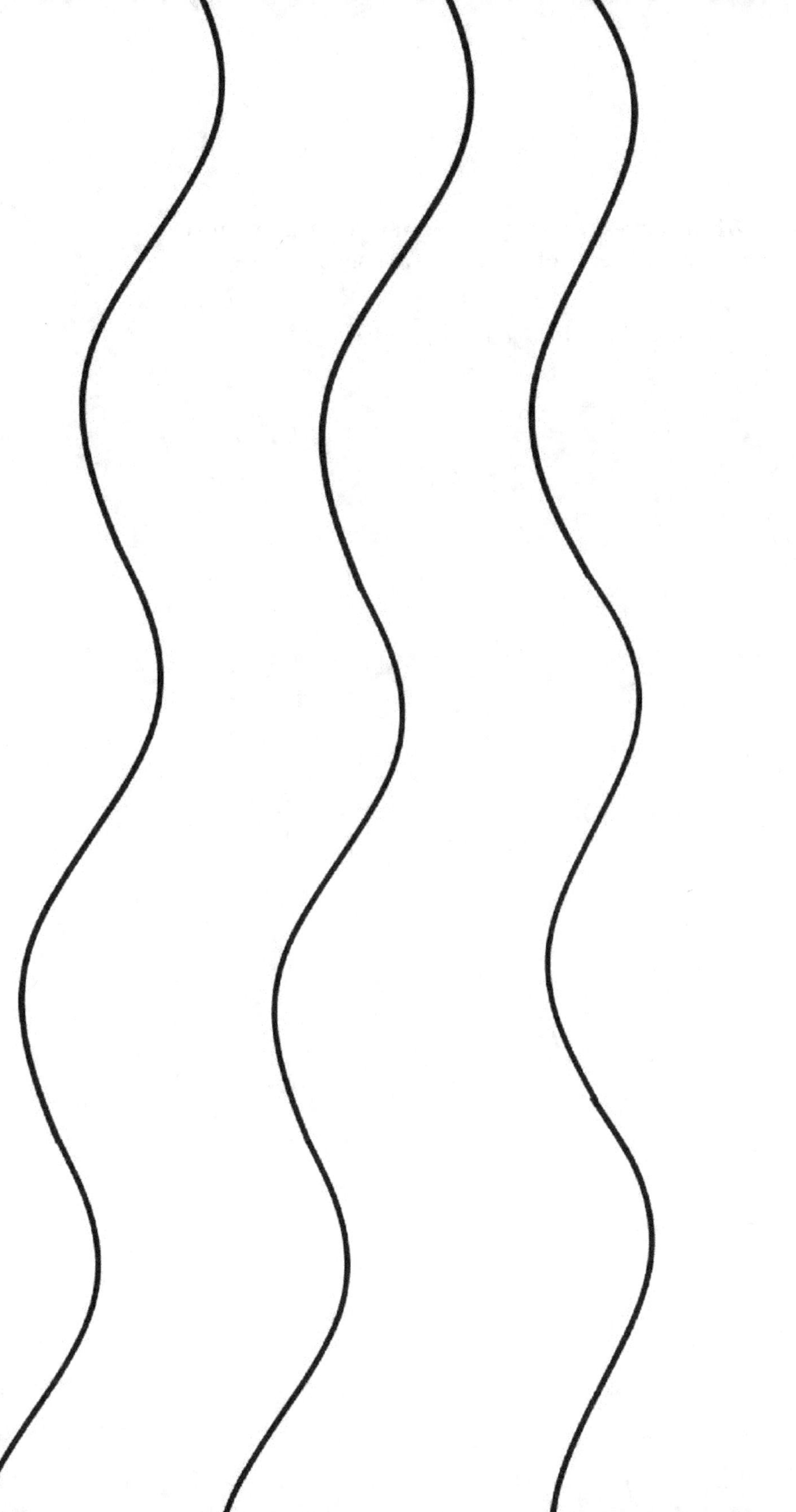

When you realize that you're losing yourself, when you
notice that pieces of you are slowly slipping away…

   - it's a grief that you can't explain

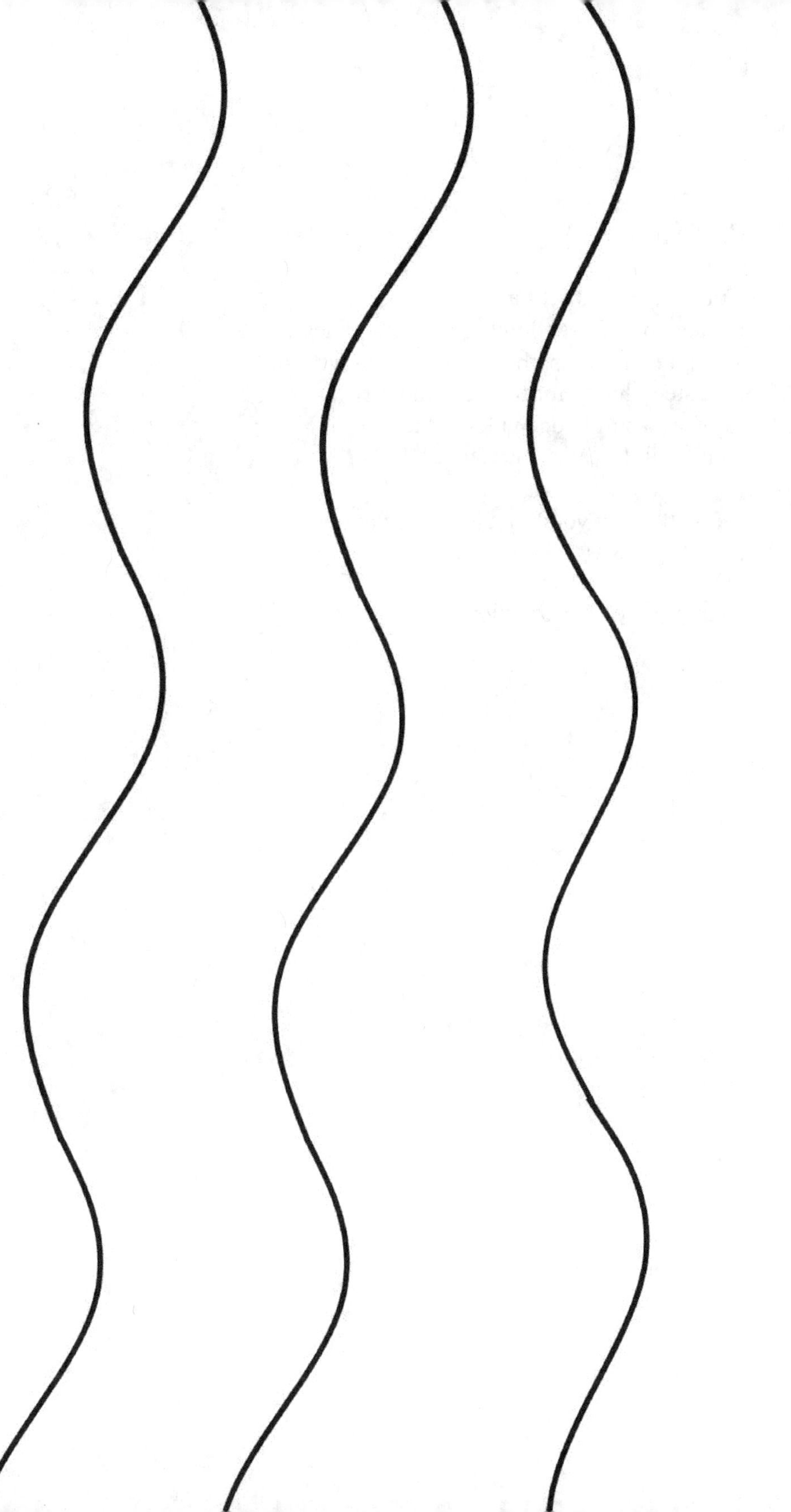

Confession

I have no idea what I am doing.
I wake up to fog and fall asleep to darkness.
My mind nor my path is clear. I'm hungry for the
next step, thirsty for the *right* move.
My feet won't budge unless I know I
won't fail. It leaves me stagnant.

I'm still in my youth but my expectations
are the same as those that are veterans. I
don't know if it's ambition or my sad
attempt to reach perfection.

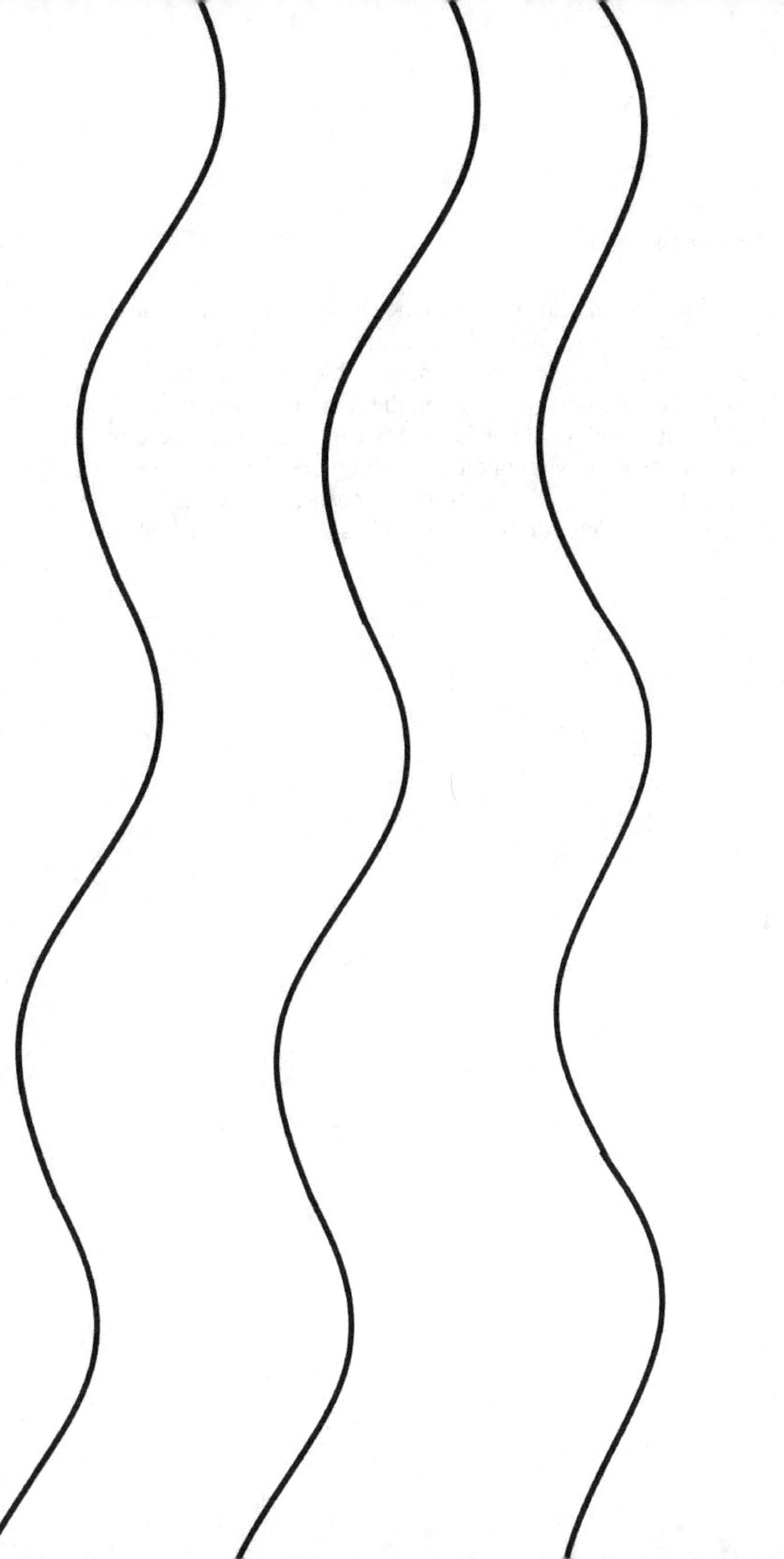

Happiness

I used to think my location was the cause of my unhappiness. I discovered the location of my happiness was the culprit. I placed my happiness in changing variables and expected it to stand when the wind blew, when the rain fell, when the sun never came, and night persisted. My happiness was placed in my conditions, it was conditional. But going through this unpredictable life where conditions constantly change, I realized, I needed it to be anchored in something immovable.

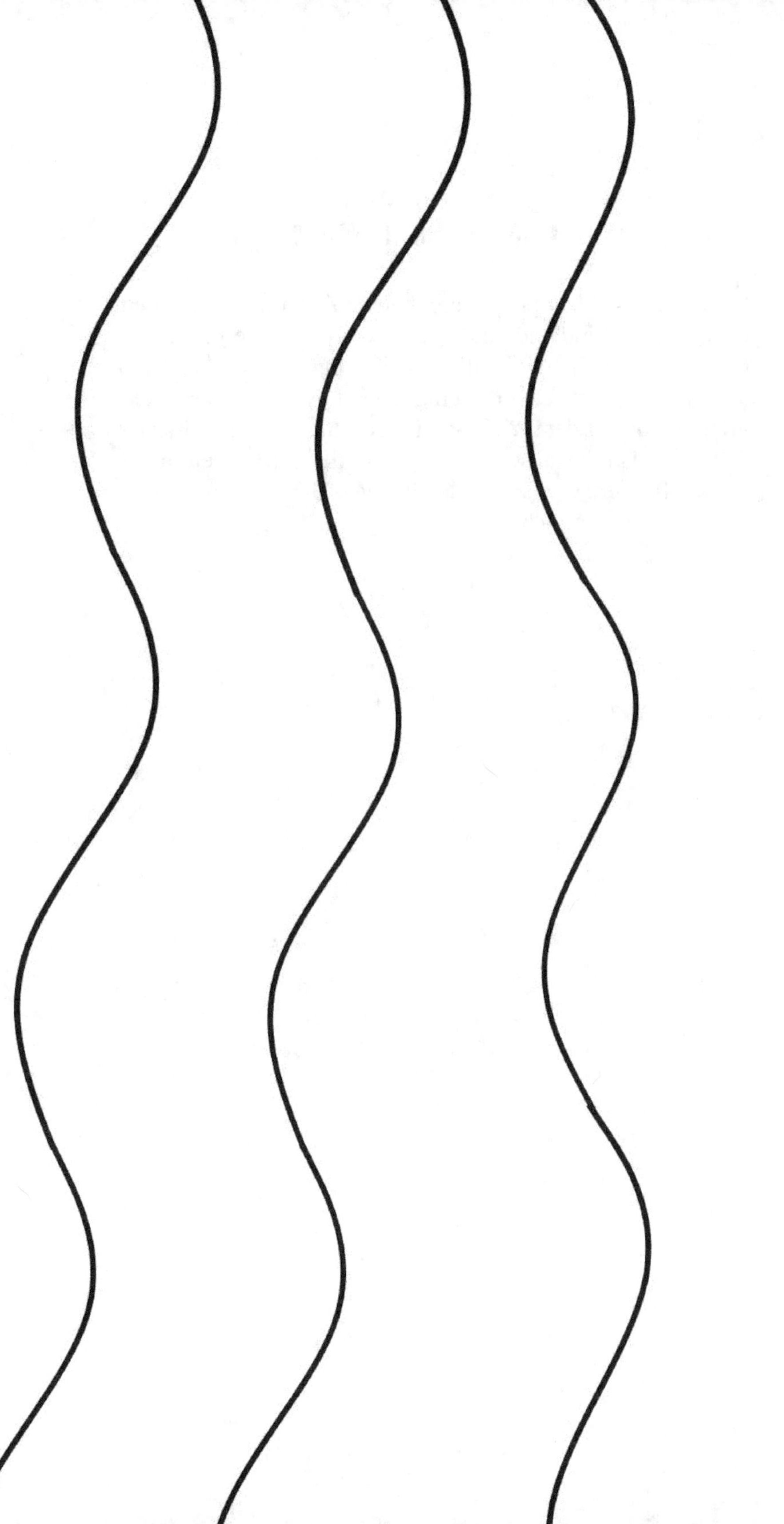

Does the soul know?

Do you think when people die their soul is in full agreement
even if their mind and body aren't ready to leave yet? Does
our soul know that it's really our time but because our minds
and bodies are capable of being tainted by fear we assume we
aren't ready for death? I'd say it does know. Then, why not
warn me? Is it because this body isn't destined for eternity?
Or is it because the body's death means the soul can be free?
Does the soul know?

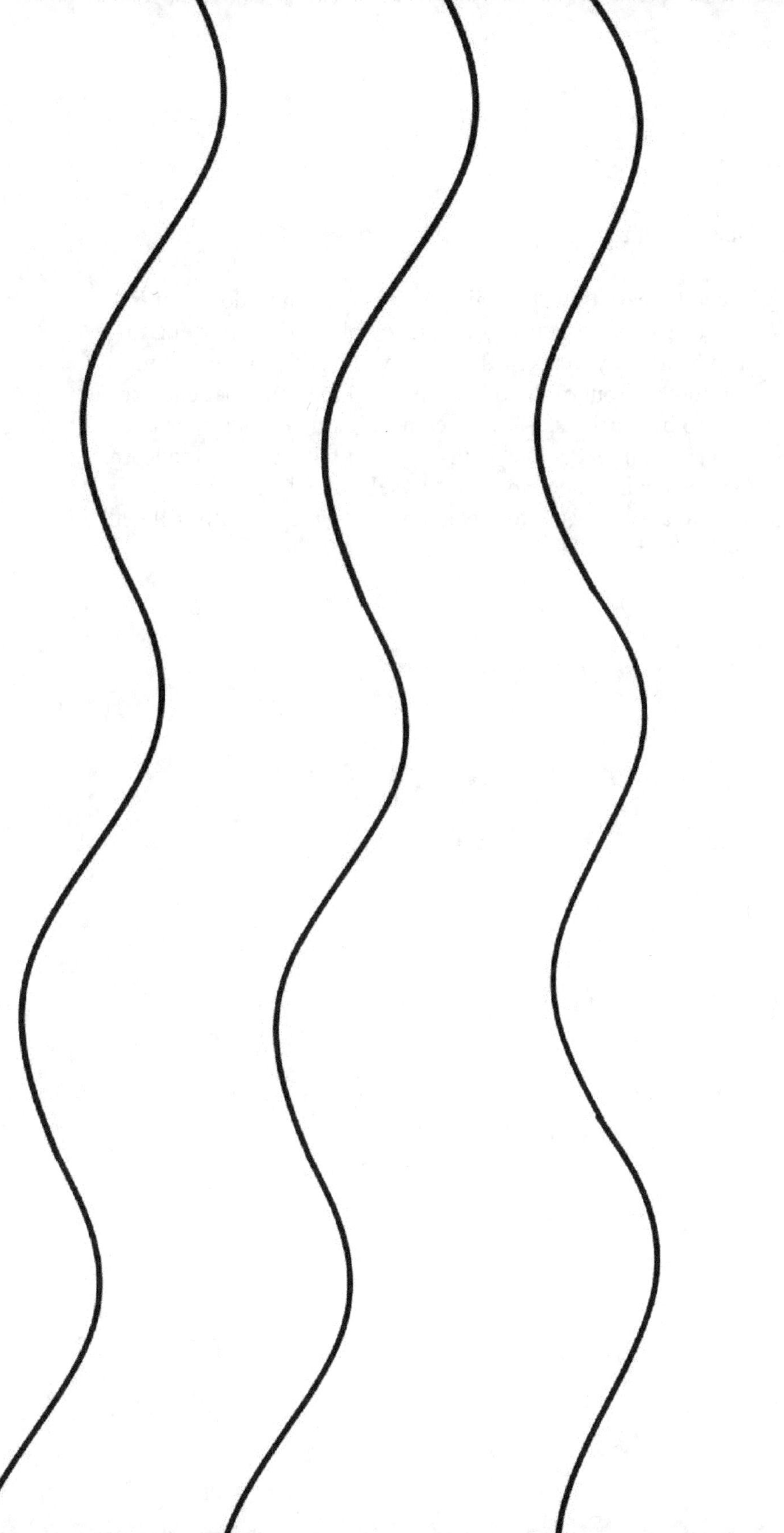

One step at a time

I need to learn to walk again. With everything I do I'm trying
to sprint. That slow paced efficiency phase, I keep trying to
skip. I'm ready to take off but I haven't even learned to put
one foot in front of the other. I haven't mastered patience or
how to be gracious. I have dreams of being on big stages but
the criticism that comes with it, I can't take it. I need to learn
to walk again. I need to allow myself to make mistakes. I
need to allow myself to break, and I know eventually I'll get
to my destined place.

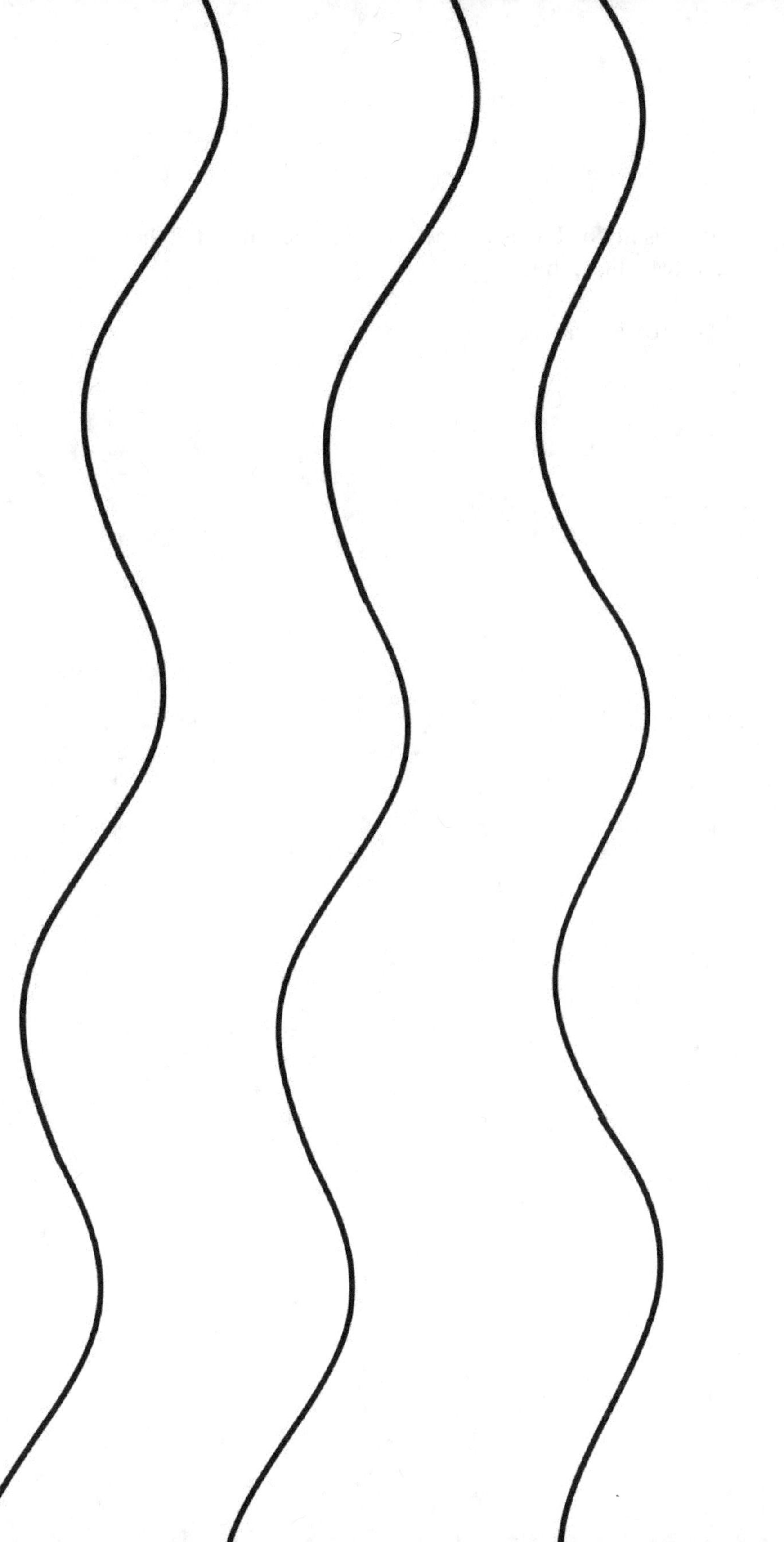

Some days my bed feels like a deserved place of rest. Other days it feels like a trap.

 - procrastinating

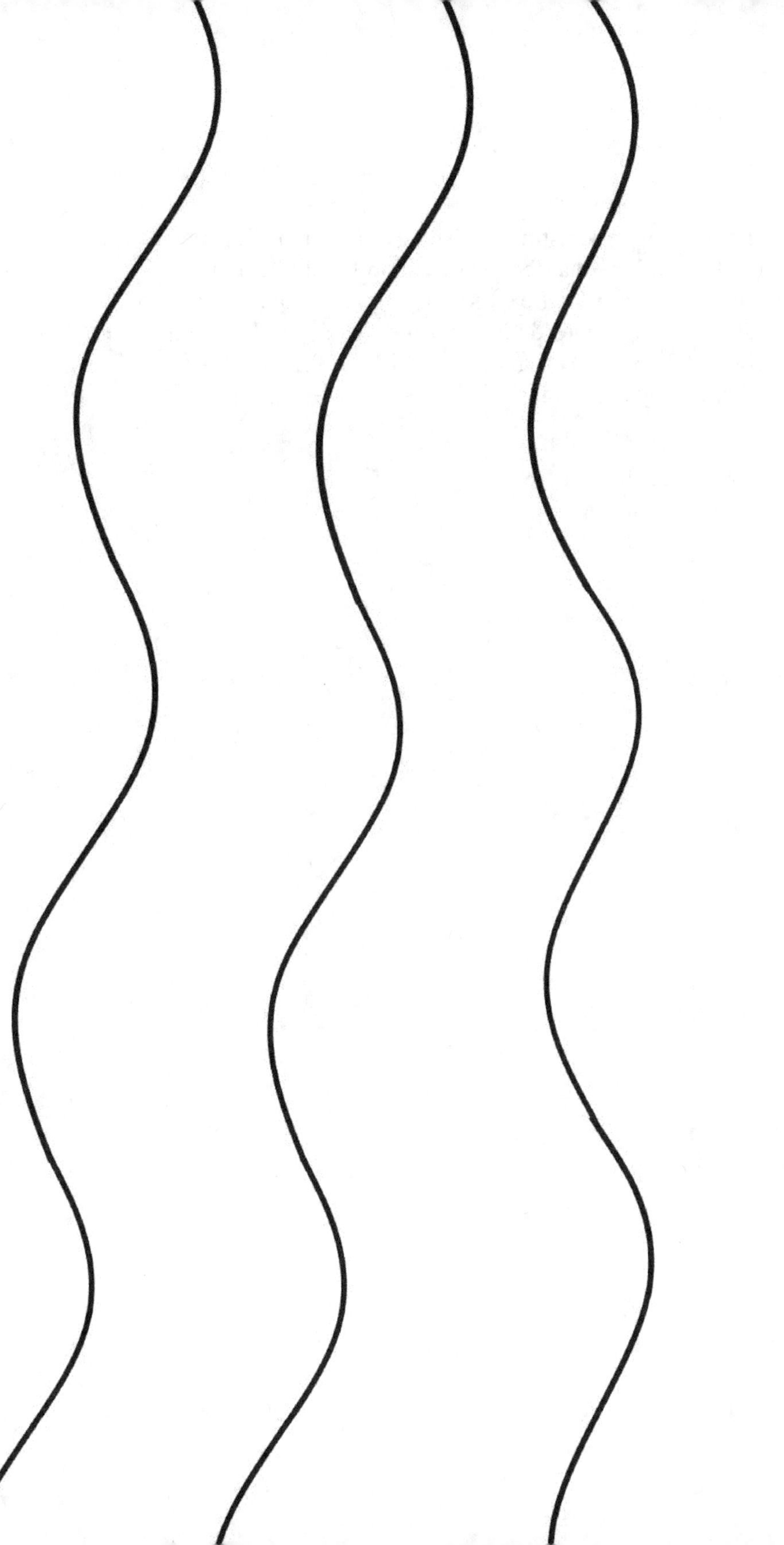

I envy how procrastination isn't even in your dictionary. I'm jealous of how that feeling of "I don't feel like it" isn't a roadblock for you. I prayed for your ambition. I prayed to stop treating my to-do list full of necessary tasks like they're optional things. You treat yours like they're the very vitals that keep you living.

    - Queen Mother

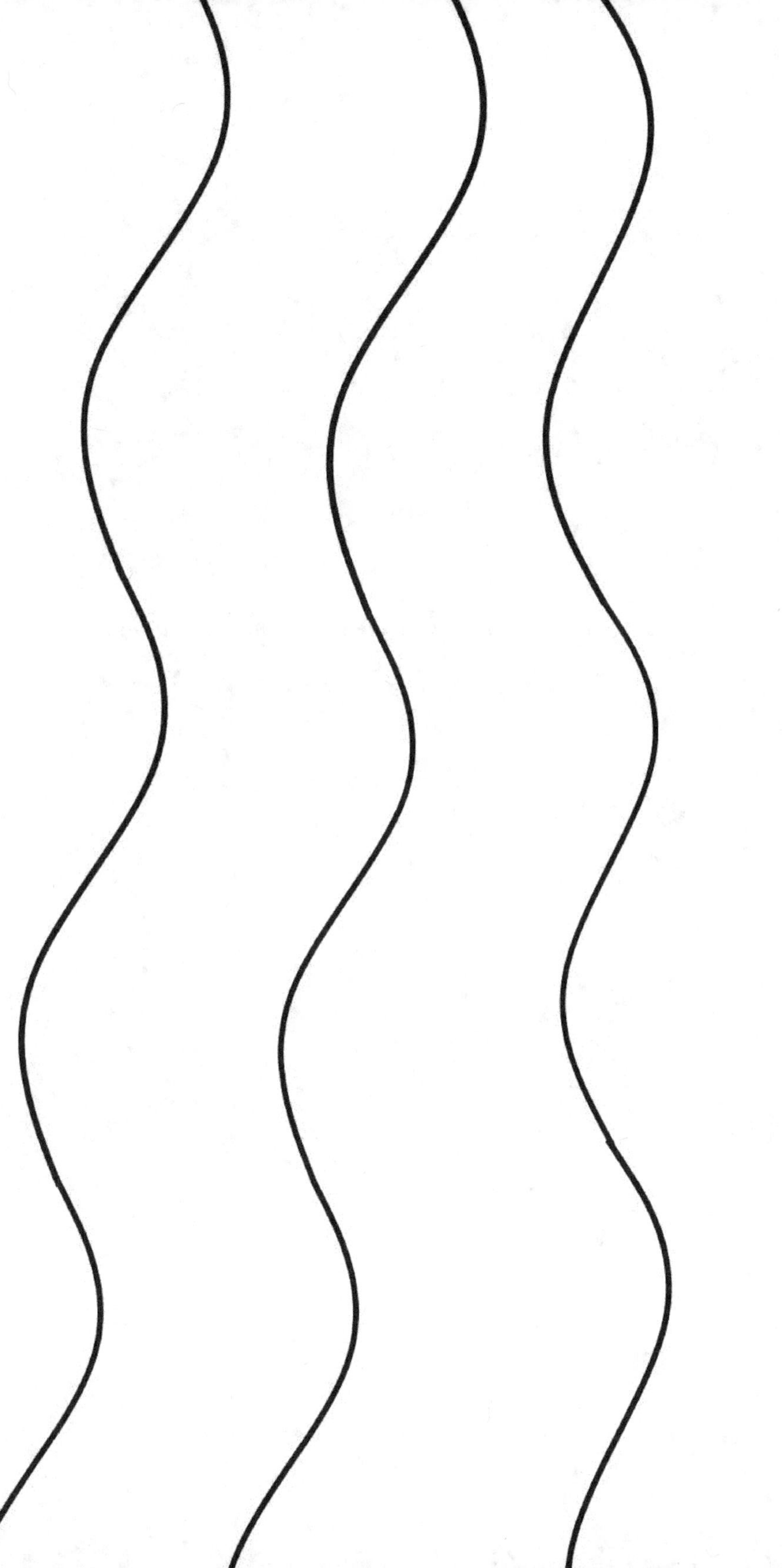

You're battered but you're the one doing the beating.

Aimlessly floating

My fear of the waters is similar to my fears in life. The
oceans and their vastness represent life's boundless
outcomes. The fear that I'll be taken by life's tides, left with
no control, nothing to grapple and no clue what these waters
hold, is the reason why I plan. It's the reason I want to know
all of life's events, big or small. It's the reason I stay close to
the shore. So I won't be left drowning or aimlessly floating.

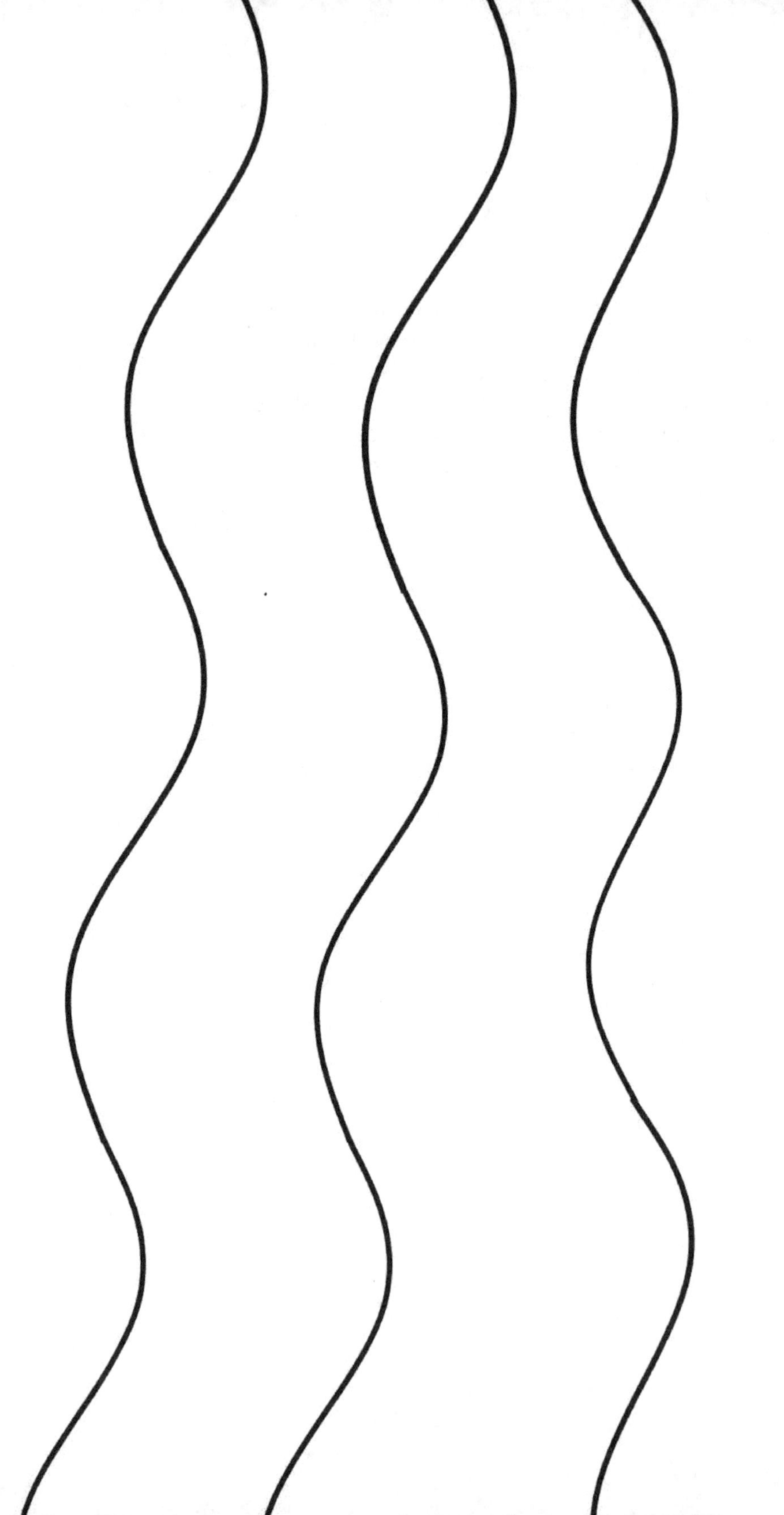

Slow down

You're so tightly wound.

Stop and smell the roses.

What is this sense of urgency?

This is a marathon but your mind keeps telling you "Run

Faster!"

Where are you going?

Don't sacrifice the journey and your happiness for your
timeline.

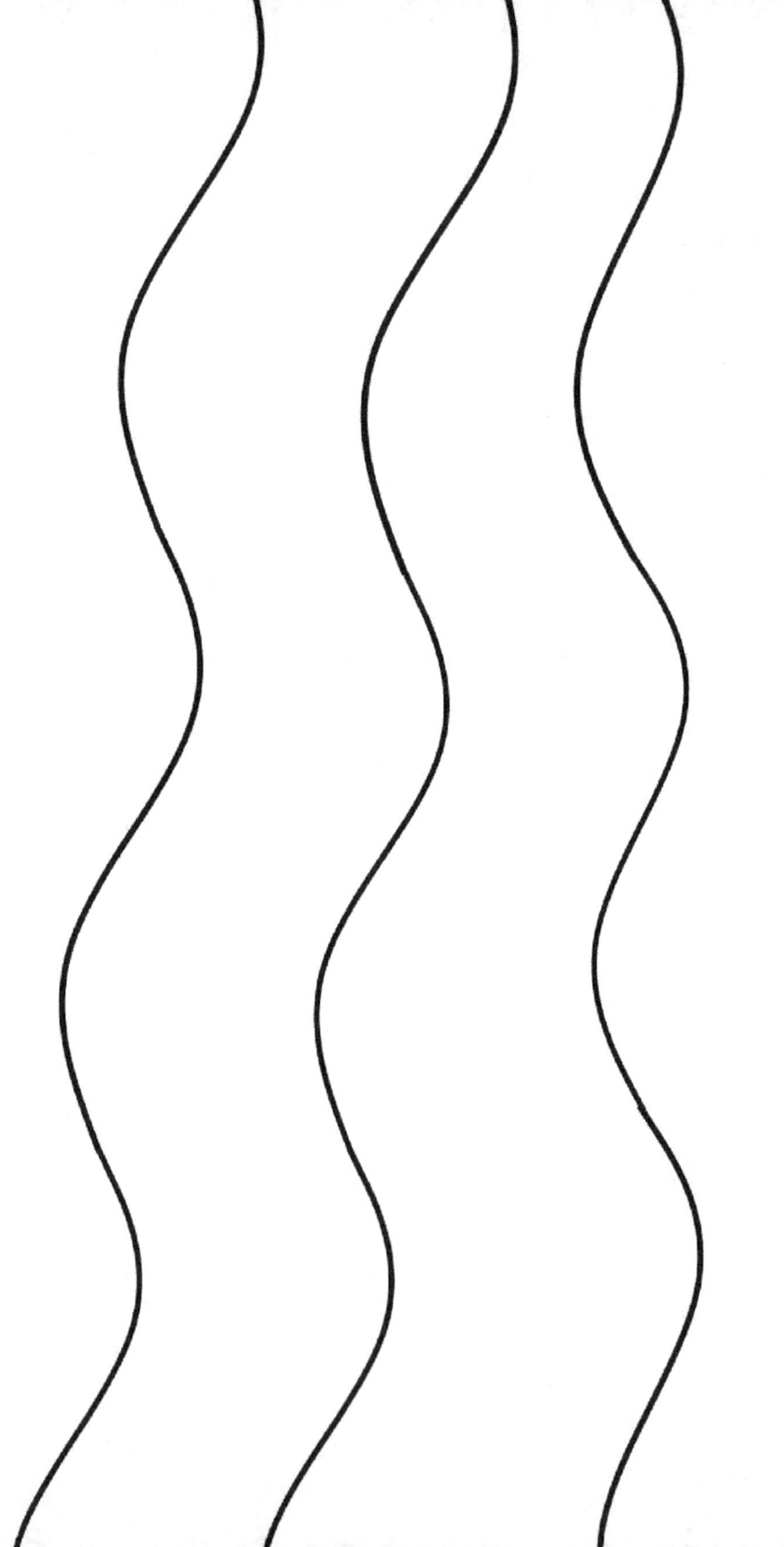

Smart girl

You don't know it

all. No one is

judging your whys

and hows.

It's okay to wonder.

It's not okay to pretend

like you have infinite

knowledge. That only

leaves you the same with

no room for gain. The

pride in pretending takes

up space. It takes up the

space where actual

knowledge could dwell.

Smart girl, yearn for

knowledge, not the need

to be right.

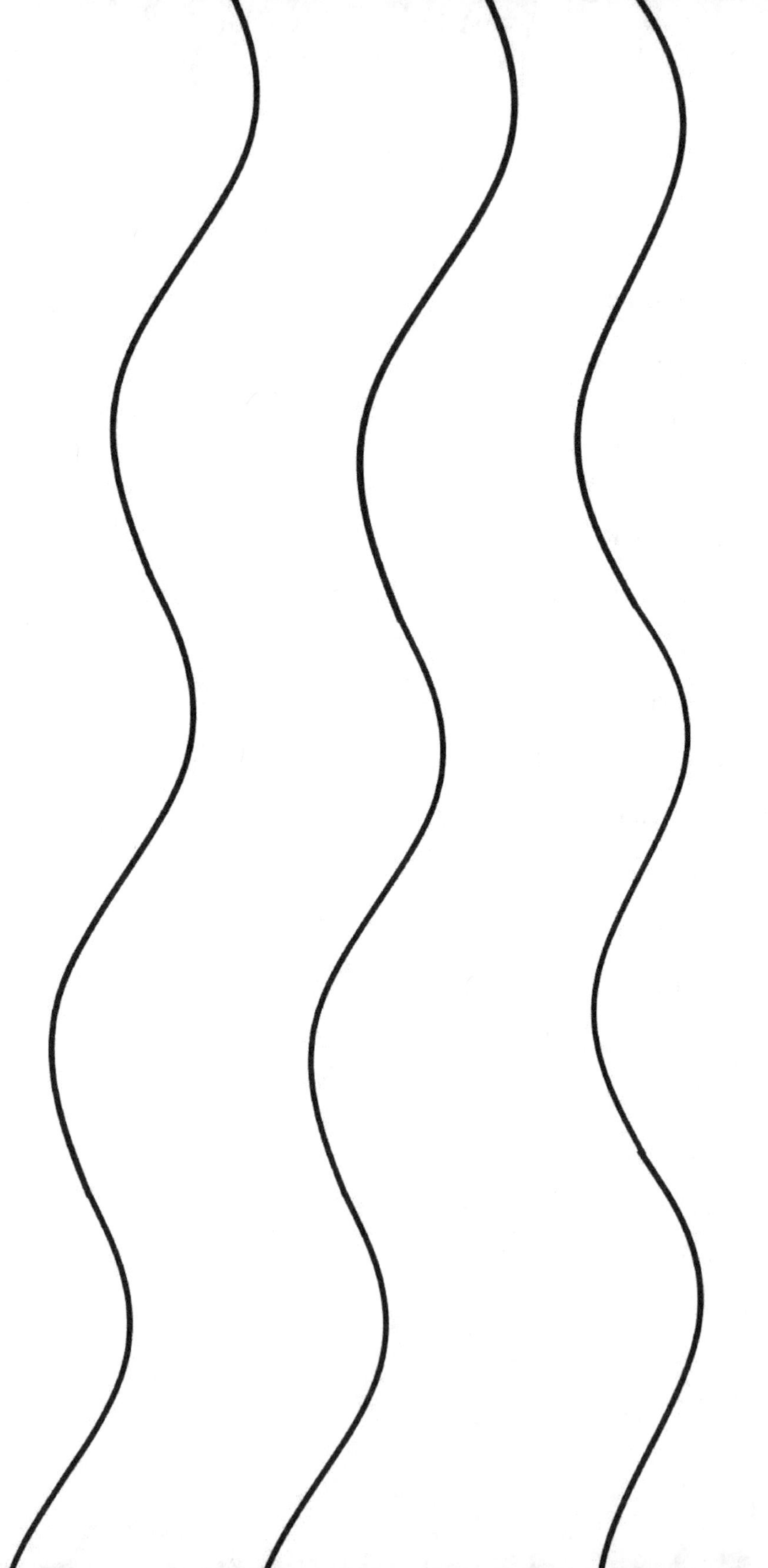

The seldom times "no" escaped my lips, it felt like it hurt me more than them.

   - people pleaser

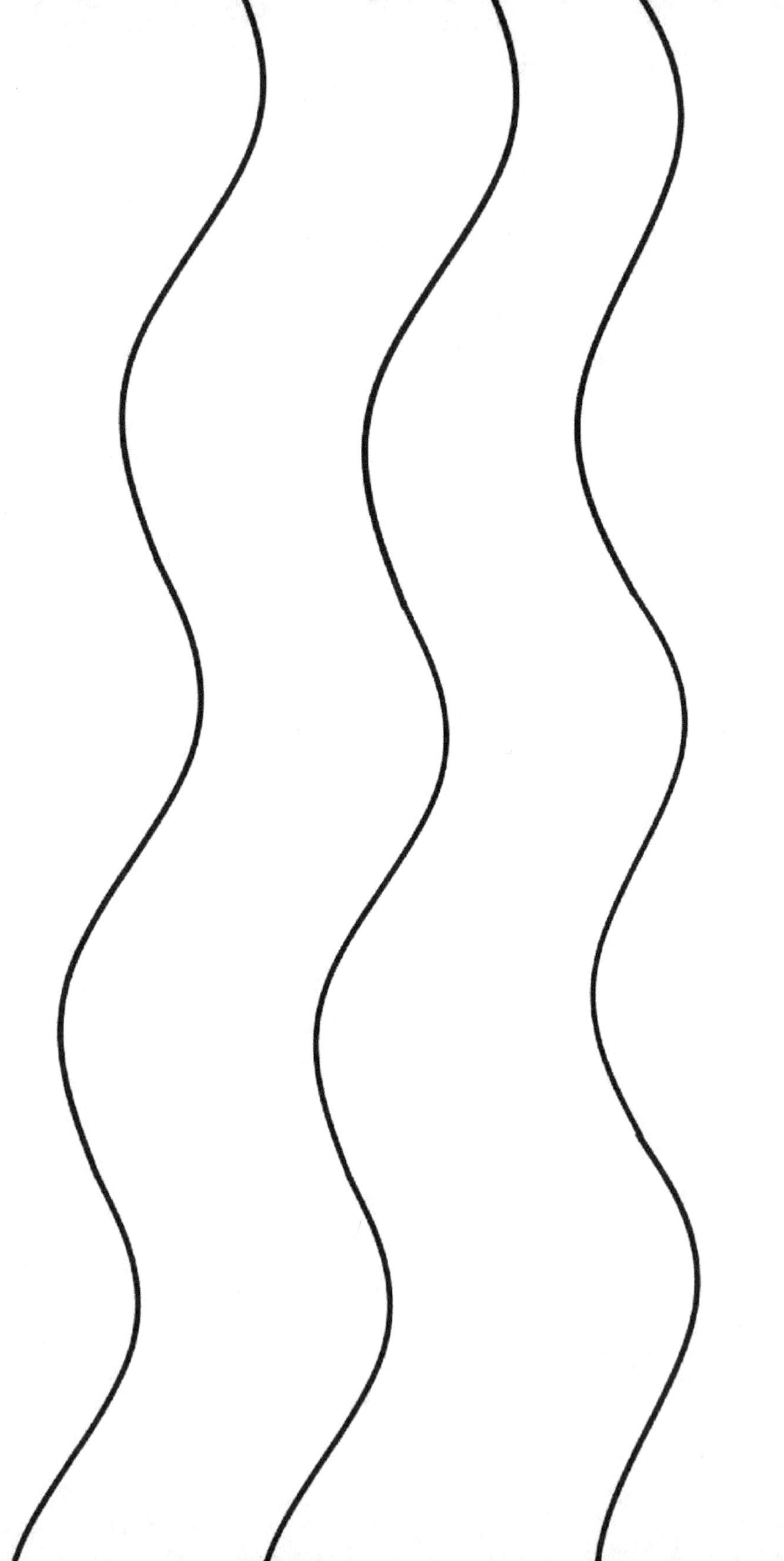

As my ink infused blood drips on these blank pages, my heart leaps, because when anxiety has my tongue imprisoned, my pen remains free.

Invisible woman

Often ignored, seldom chosen, she keeps to herself to avoid
being broken. She becomes distant in an instant, she's
change resistant. If you're looking for her value you
probably missed it, because when she spoke you joked about
her outer appearance. Her value was in her words, some too
impatient to listen. An active imagination, she's truly gifted.
Invisible at times but gems are meant to be hidden.

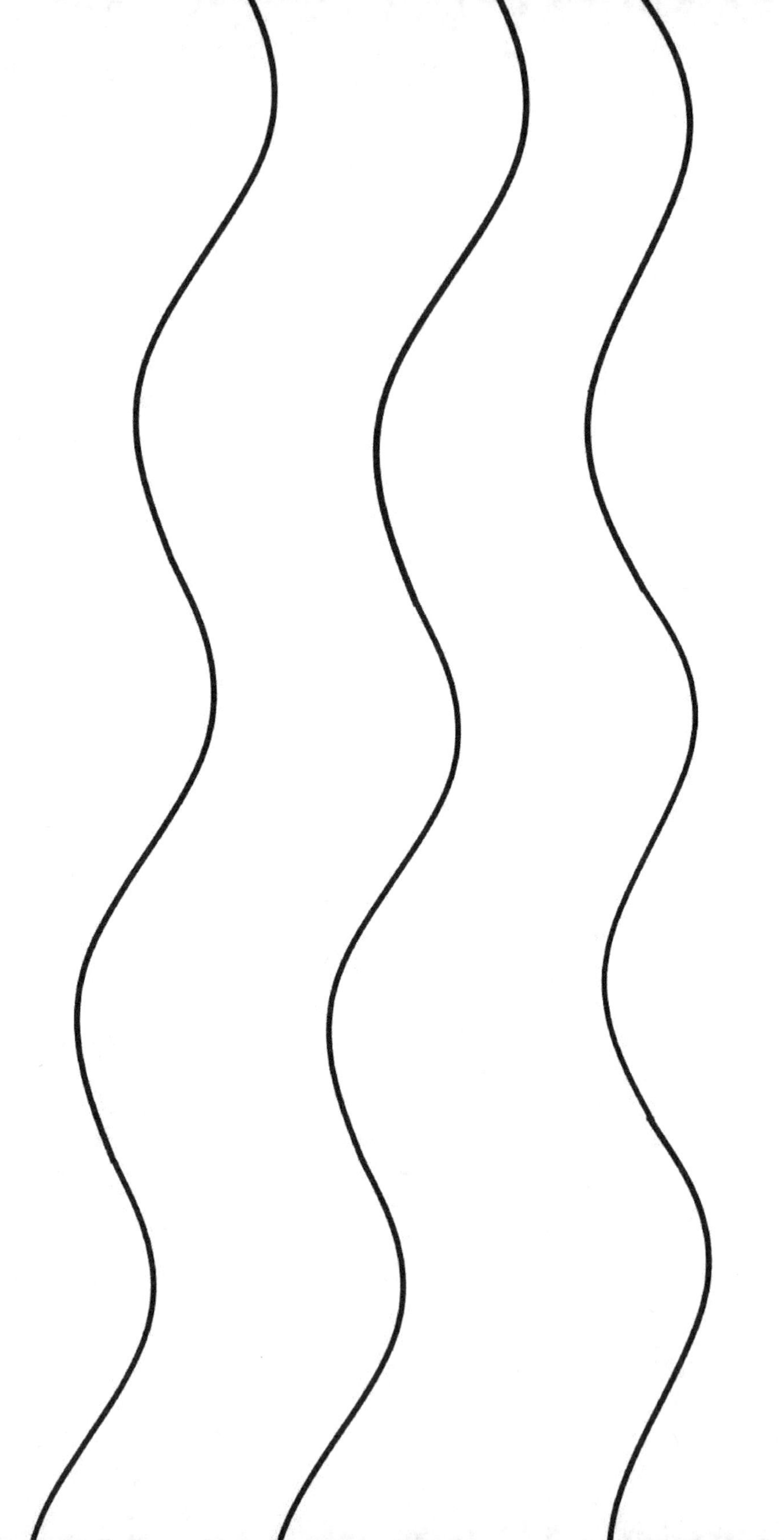

Words create worlds

"Words create worlds."
"Life and death lies in the power of the tongue."
"What you say is what you get."

Whichever way you say it, the meaning doesn't change. This philosophy is engraved on the heart of my mother, and I've seen its workings in the lives of my brothers. There's no doubt of its power. Since a young age I've watched my words, and I enjoyed the pictures they've painted. But when pain gained my attention, I began speaking its language.

I uttered phrases that would've brought tears to my father's eyes. I spoke in paragraphs about how I no longer wanted to be alive. No matter how many ways I thought about doing it, I couldn't go through with it. Then this philosophy entered my view again.

I was sent a video by my sibling with the title, "Words create worlds." I knew I was under fear's arrest, so I decided to put this philosophy to the test. I sprinkled my speech with suicide like it was a garnish because I *wanted* these words to create a world. I wanted them to create a world I was no longer in. So, if this philosophy was true, it would do what I didn't have the courage to do. But everything I spoke came back void.

That doesn't discredit these teachings that were taught to me. I simply believe when I called for death, the call was left unanswered because there were other words spoken over me before I came to be. Words of promise and purpose. Words of life. Words that came before the tears, heartache, grief, and strife. I believe these words cannot return void because of who spoke them. I believe the words in my story have to come to pass because of who wrote them.

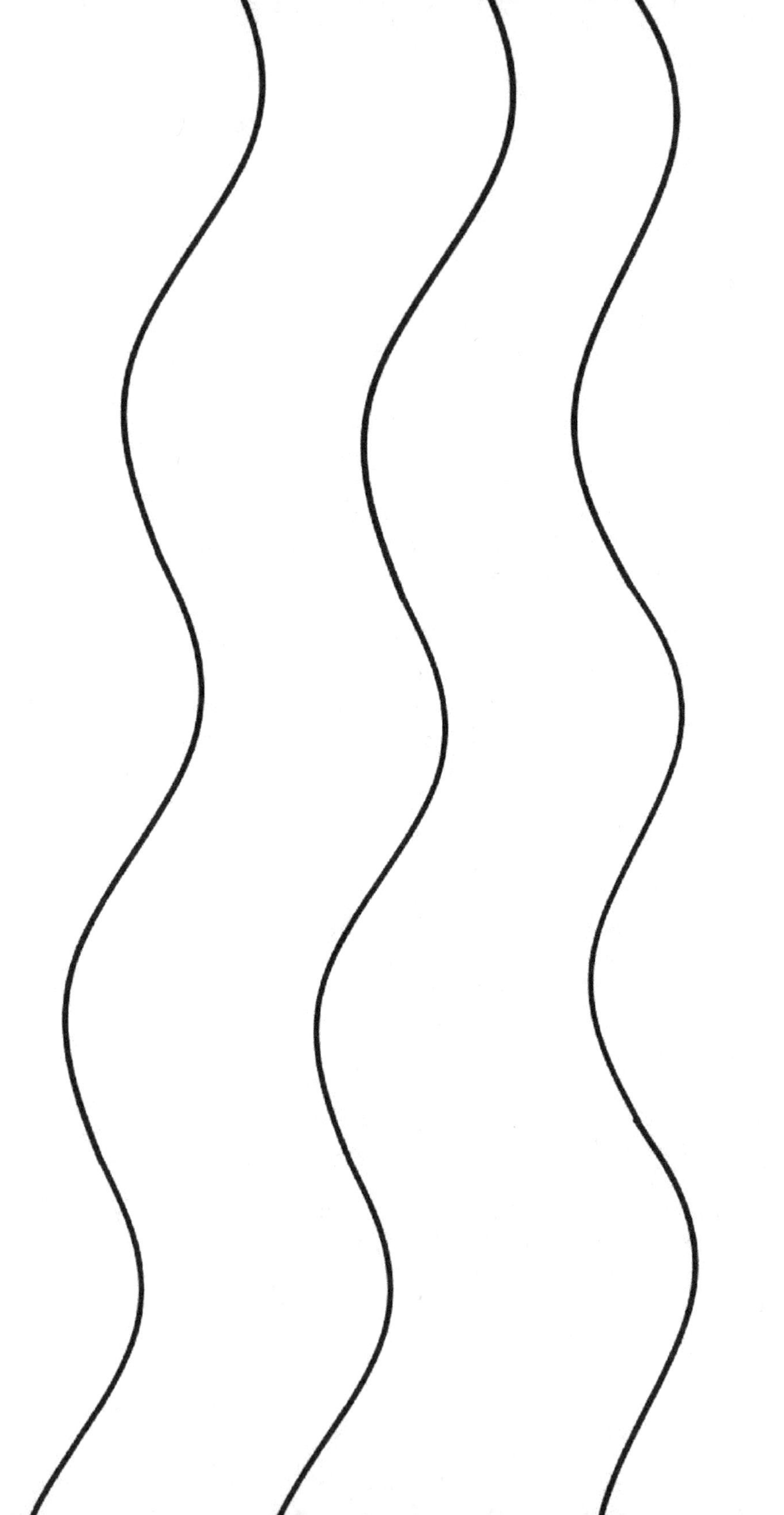

Consider their emotions, whether you understand them or
not. Give them grace. Confirm their existence. Let them
know they belong here.

   - how to save a life

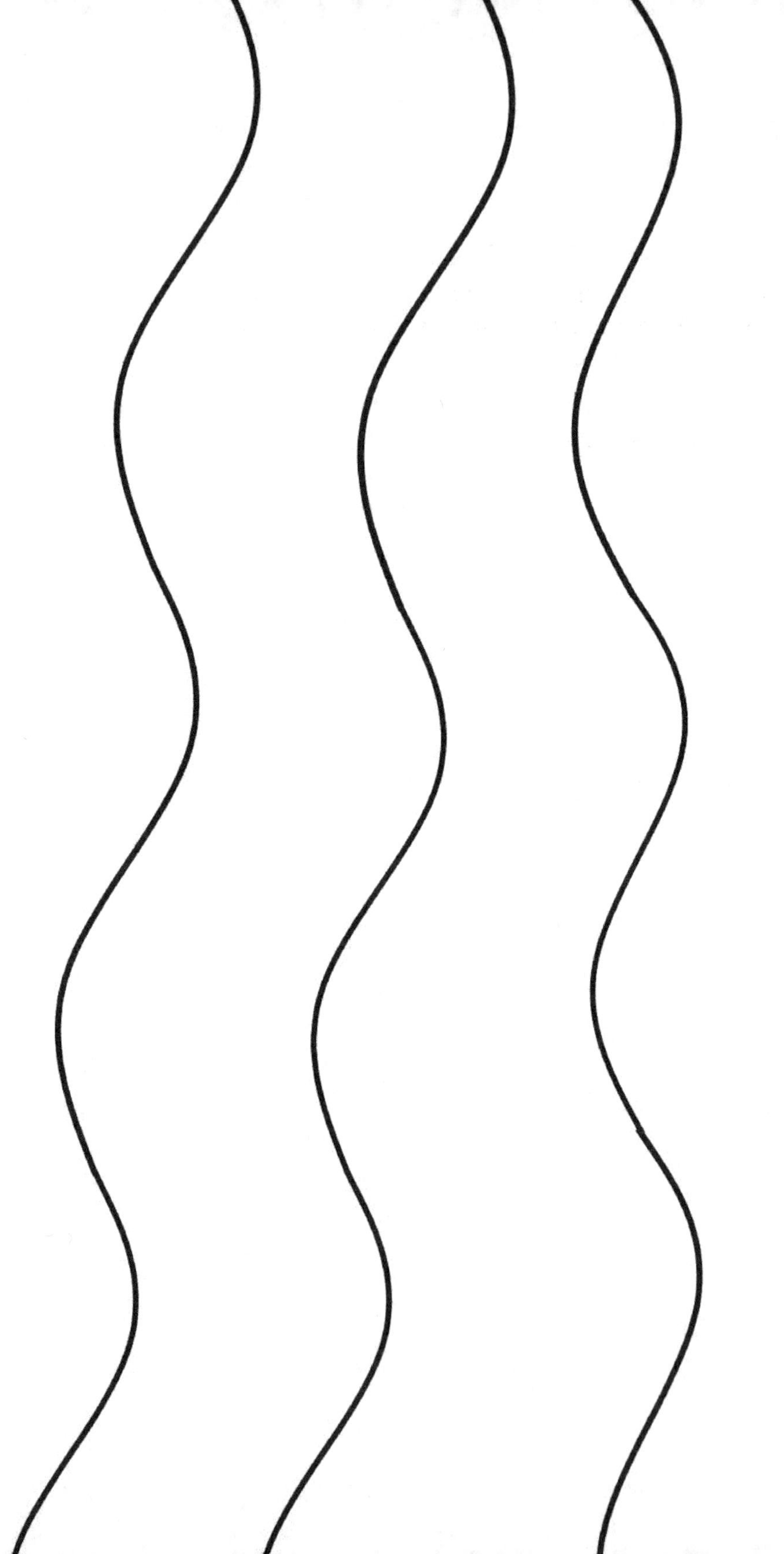

I said a prayer today. I wonder where it went. The words leapt from my lips with so much confidence. With every syllable I spoke, my soul cheered. With everything I laid bare, my mind cleared. In that moment doubt had no residencies and faith had no vacancies. My heart and mind were in agreement that anything I had asked, that is willed, could never miss me.

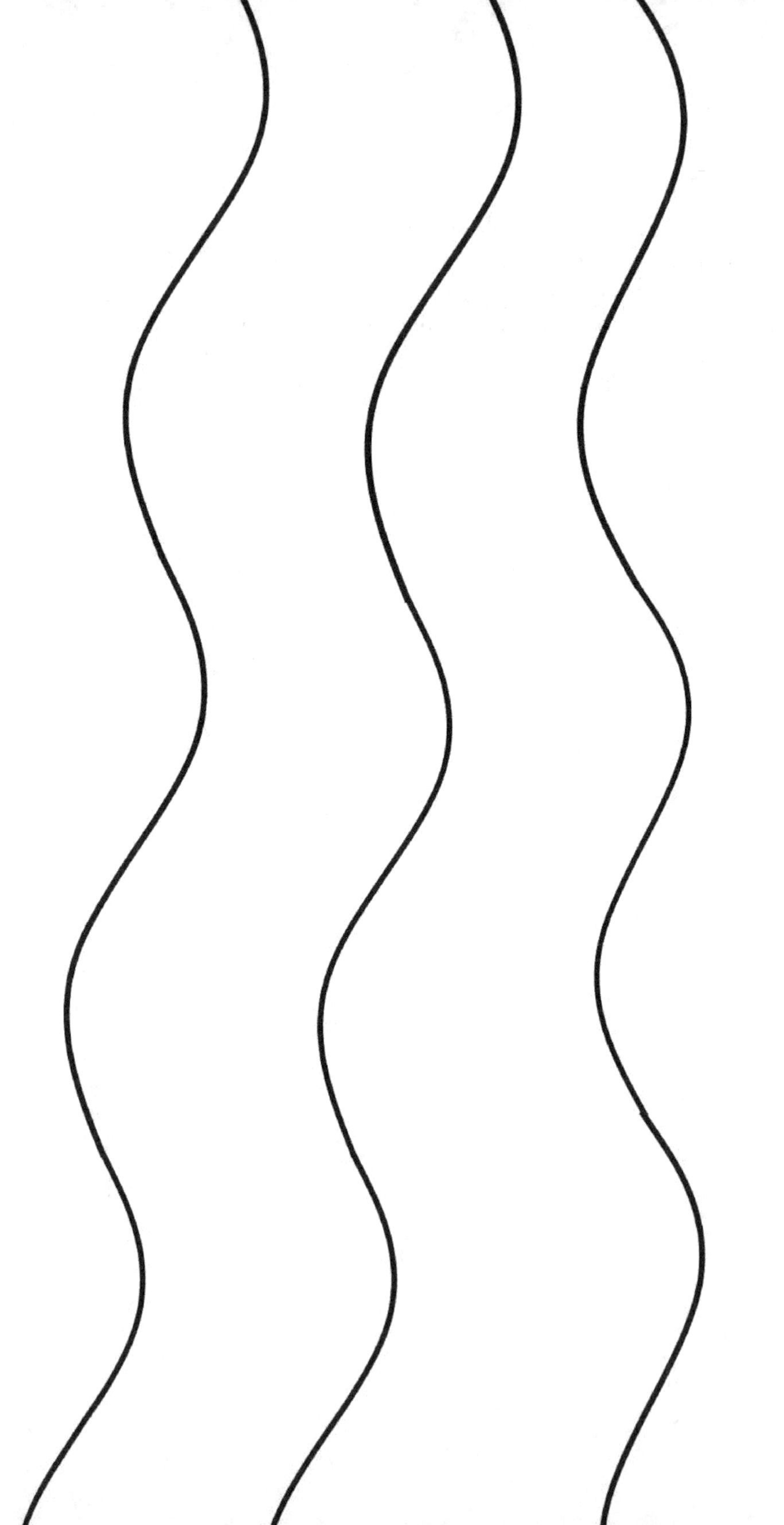

The girl I wish to be

Her days start with prayer.

Gratitude drips from her lips.

Her temple is mentally and physically undefiled.

Her most important relationships

are well watered and flourishes even in tribulation.

She's partnered with grace.

She's partnered with purpose.

Even the breaths she takes are

taken with intention.

She's constantly gaining knowledge

and peace as she restores the world.

Selfish and selfless. She's mastered the balance.

She caterers to love so when the time comes for reaping, they

won't forget what she sowed. She takes her rest seriously.

Making sure to recharge and be the light she was created to
be.

- the girl I wish to be

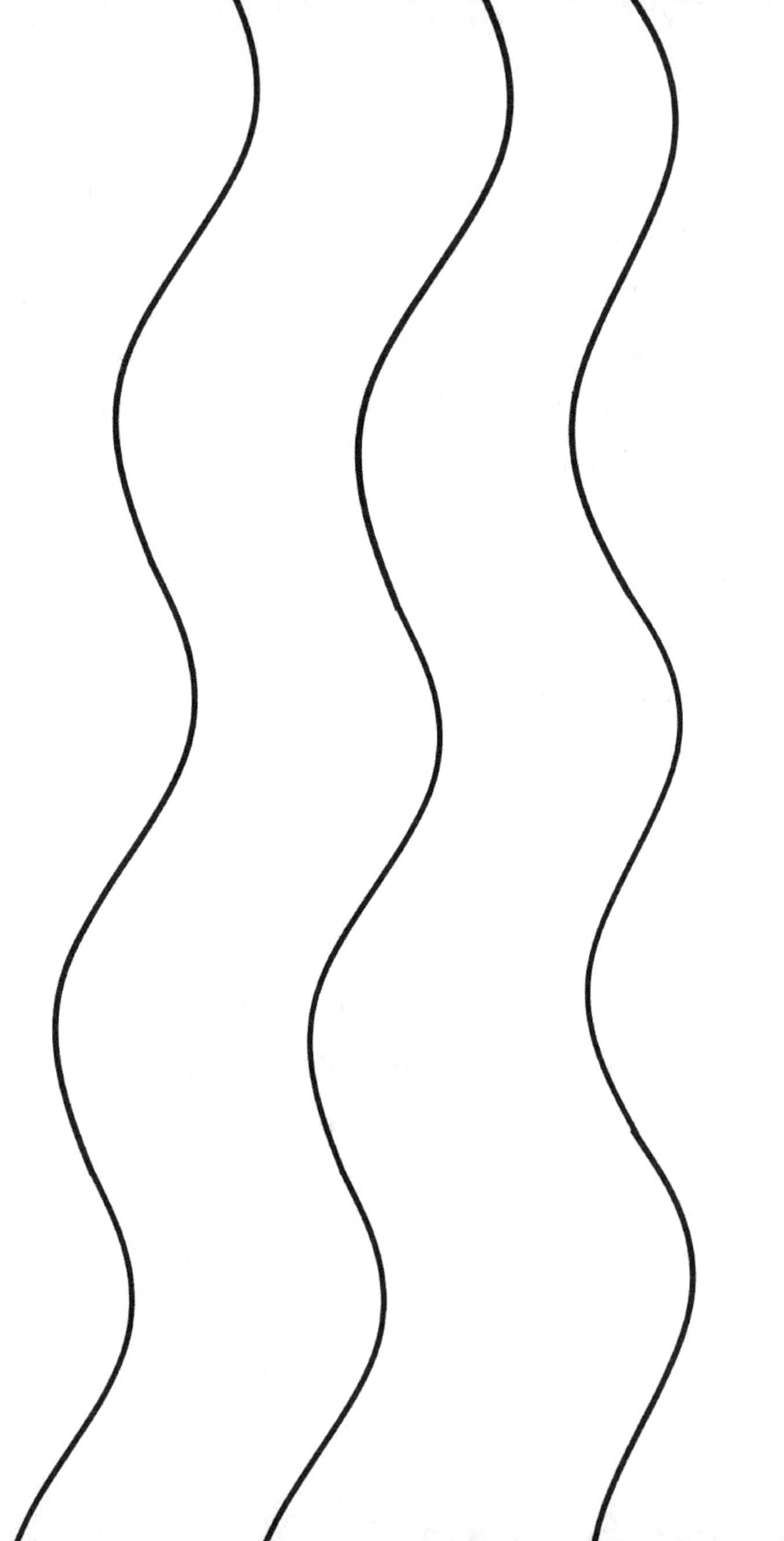

A Satisfied soul

When death stretches out her arms to take me in, my heart won't tremble if in the end I can feel the warmth of completeness. I'd accept my fate with a smile on my face. If everything that God wrote and spoke has been checked off and my feet have entered rooms where my presence was destined, she can have me. I won't resist. If my name was a sweet taste amongst my peers and a serene sound to the right ears and a bitter taste to everything that opposed me and a dreadful sound to my enemies, then death can come for me. I'd walk happily into her embrace.

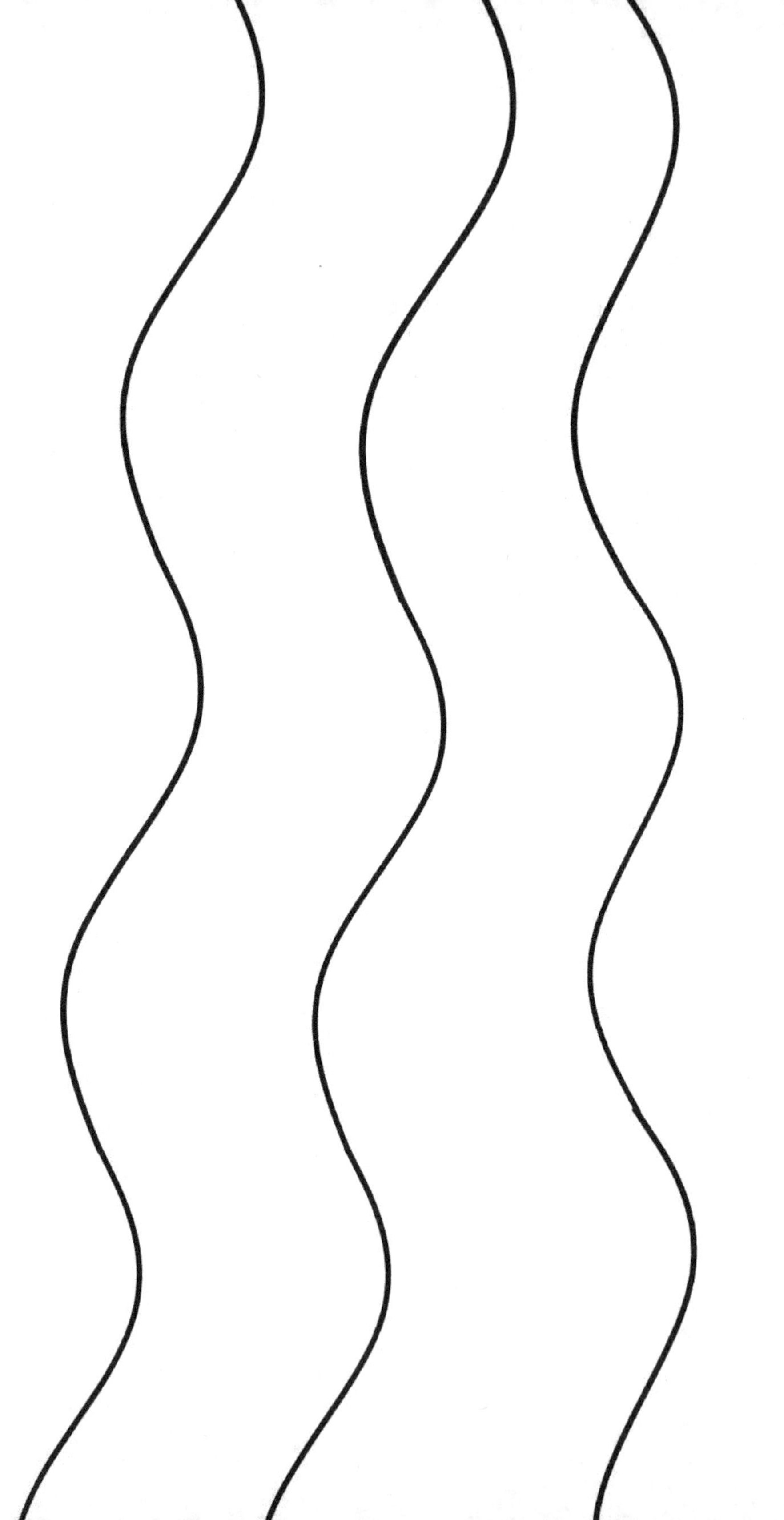

Hope

My hope renews with the days.

My nights tend to be the darkest. Listening ears would only hear the sound of my heart aching and my screams as I suffer the abuse of frustration. Despair wreaks havoc taking over my mind as it pressures me to give in, but just as I'm at my wit's end, the sun comes.

My mornings tend to be brightest. The light eradicates the night's damage. It causes me to not recall the pain I felt when darkness surrounded me. The light reminds me where my hope resides, In the things I can be and in the things God wants me to see, that's where my hope lies.

My hope renews with the days.

So as long as God has willed the sun to set and rise, that's how long I'll have hope in my eyes.

Welcome to Rock Bottom

I broke down and discovered there was
a place beneath rock bottom. It was filled
with reflections. My <u>flaws</u> laid uncovered
ready to be dissected.

* *Flaws: emotion stifling, toxic generational behaviors, anger, & negative self talk etc*

As my resentment for the place swelled
so did my contentment. Despite my hatred
for this sorrow filled palace,I saw <u>generational burdens</u> being lifted.

* I met my darkness.
Its hold on me was vicious. At first it was a nuisance
but the deeper I got the more I felt its chains loosen.

"I met my darkness" Darkness = Past Things that happened before me. I met the anger my ancestors harbored and passed down. I met the toughness that life forced upon my mother. I looked it in its eyes. It promised me I'd feel no pain. That I'd experience life with no emotions. It offered me emotional numbness and disguised it as "resiliency." I rejected its offer.

The pressure and frustration forced my unhealthy habits to come the front line and I had to deal with them. These were things I'd seen my parents struggle with mentally and emotionally.

Breathe into me

Wake me up!
I lay here lifeless, hoping I could awake and live!
I'm envious of Adam. Breathe into me with the same
devotion you had with him. Become my barterer.
Take these ashes and give me beauty!

I felt like a body with
no life. No passion, no
emotions, & no future in
sight. I Felt lifeless. My
place of rest became my
habitat. I called for a
wind, for a
resuscitation. I wanted
myself back. I wanted
my passions back but
depression had it all in a
headlock.

* Spirit, life, wind

Frustration

Come undone

In moments of laughter only a grin is present. In the heat of your anger words
fail to walk off your tongue but the tears never cease to run. And in the depths
of frustration and undeniable pressure you still refuse to come undone. In your
trials of sadness and sickness, God was your only witness. A helping hand
couldn't attest, because in every situation you were the good samaritan coming
to help yourself. In the presence of company, you act as the observer. You notice
every change of emotion, the fake smiles covering things that are broken and
your ear is tuned to the warning signs of commotion. In the face of freedom you
refuse its invitation because inhibition is your habitation. In this analogy you are
the dam waiting to burst. In this human life the chances of you allowing
yourself to be human are next to none. You can hear your inner being screaming
come undone!

* My happy moments looks different from the usual. I acknowledge it, yes, but I move on. I don't express that feeling of happiness. I don't know why, maybe because I'm not use to being celebrated. Maybe all my accomplishments weren't given the excite they should have been given. I don't know.

* My moments of anger are never expressed. Or even acknowledged. Suppress, Suppress, Suppress. Despite the pressure and pain I feel in my body when I'm doing it, I don't stop. I'm ashamed of my anger. I don't know why. Maybe it's because my anger was always condemned growing up instead of being processed. I don't know.

* My sad moments are only for me. I'm a master at hiding my sadness. Maybe that's why I can see when others do it. "I'm okay" is the only response I give to my sadness. I don't why. Maybe because I was never taught how to handle those moments. I don't know.

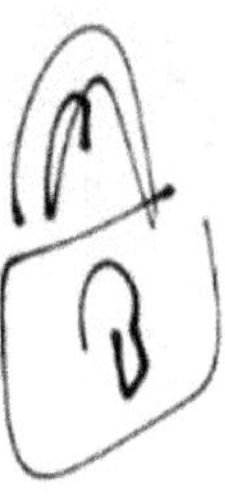

I wish I could mourn in the morning

I wish the tears that fell when the moon
and stars were shining appeared after the sun
had finished rising. I wish my depression didn't cower.
I wish it had the courage to show its face when all eyes were on me. Instead it
waits until the only thing looking is darkness. It waits until help is far gone and
no matter how loud my wails are, they will be left unanswered. It waits until the
only thing there to catch my tears are pillows.

* I could have wrote a book about how
I needed help but my "I'm okay"
mentality would have rewrote it. All the
stories of my
tears would have been replaced. The
stories of my sleepless nights would be
replaced. The reader wouldn't have
known what was going on behind close
doors because I'd hide it. I'm glad
I'm learning. I'm glad I'm learning
to tell people about this anger, about
this sadness, about this frustration.